# FIND A WAY TO MAKE A WAY!

**You're Either Part of the Problem, or You're Part of the Solution.**

**H.S. Reed, Jr.**

This book is a goldmine of inspirational quotes, entertaining, and great ideas in which we all are either a part of the problem or a part of the solution. I myself have already purchased six copies and given them to professional athletes, college athletes, professional businessmen, and family members for gifts. I would highly recommend Reed's book to everyone. This book that I have read two times helped me put a fire back into my own life at fifty-two years of age. This helped re-inspire my confidence and helped me realize and believe that the future starts today. A real page turner!

—C. Grimsley, Atlanta, GA (Author of The White Golden Bull)

In this day and age, people are searching for significance, value, and purpose in life. In Find a Way to Make a Way! Reed empowers readers to know that if the work, drive, and desire is put forth, one can achieve anything that they desire and more. In the book, Lesson Two begins with "Life Gives You What You Ask It," so one is left with no other choice but to ask themselves "What am I asking of life?" Reed has literally brought back the full essence of the meaning of a self-help book!

—K. Long, Denver, CO (Founder and Lead Wholeness Advisor of The Wholeness Group, LLC)

Find a Way to Make a Way! is not your average motivational book. Reed forces you to take accountability for any and all shortcomings you may have had in the past. With accountability you can then take charge to make a way. If you are looking for a kick in the pants to change your life, this is the book for you.

—R. Taylor, Bronx, NY (Web Development Director, Qatalyst Design Inc.)

I know there are a lot of self-help books out there, but this book is truly different! You are immediately challenged to sign a contract with yourself and the author to commit to making a serious change with your life. This book is definitely not for the weak at heart or those who are not committed to making a change for the better. I have become an investor in my own human spirit! Watch out for those bubble busters! Kudos to Mr. Reed! I cannot wait for his next book!

—P. Webster-Grant, Philadelphia, PA

This book truly takes you through a journey. After only reading the first few chapters, I could see that Reed really knows how to make you think outside the box by not just pursuing your goals but rather committing to completing them.

—M.G. Diggs, Plainfield, NJ

My daughter, who is twenty-eight, and my son, twenty-three, really enjoyed reading this book. They actually took the book before I could read it. My daughter stated the reading is real and refreshing. She explained that everything was described in a detailed way that she can really relate to. She told her brother that he may not be quite ready to explore all of the experiences but he should hold on to the book for future reference. I have bought several copies for my family members to assist them with their continued growth and development as well.

—A. Jones, East Orange, NJ

Find a Way to Make a Way! was a great help to me. I especially liked the chapter on bubble busters. It basically says that there will be people in your life that will tell you that you can't. Not because they don't want you to but because they really don't think you can. It also tells you that you should use their negative and turn it into a positive. Prove not to them that you can do it, but prove it to yourself that you can.

—J. Francis, New York City, NY

I have to admit when I bought this book it was on the strength of my friendship with Reed. I have to admit, I have never been much of a reader. I have bought several books over the years but never got to the point of finishing them. This year I decided to try to get through at least one. Ultimately, I decided that this book would be a good place to start. On the first day I got through roughly sixty-three pages. So, I then figured if I read sixty-three pages a day I would finish the book in 3.8 days. When I finished reading, I realized that I was my biggest bubble buster. Reed's words have inspired me to do better working on me so I can better those around me.

—G. Stewart, Miami, FL

Reed's book is an exceptional piece of writing. It ushers you into the heart of finding a way and coming up with solutions as opposed to making excuses. This is an amazing story that will challenge you to live up to your highest potential.

—P. Pasteur, Central Jersey, NJ

**This book Is Dedicated To:**

My beautiful wife, Taria, who has always had my back even when there were times I did not deserve it, and to my two wonderful children, who I hope will read these words and apply themselves to greatness a lifetime sooner than I did. My parents and grandparents, who taught me about struggle and who taught me how to love.

I also wish to dedicate this book to my teachers (in alphabetical order): Les Brown, Dale Carnegie, George S. Classon, Karen Copeland, Farrah Gray, Robert Greene, Napoleon Hill, Sis. Patricia Hogan, Robert T. Kiyosaki, George LaTorre, Anthony Robbins, Brian Tracy, Sun Tzu, and (last but by no means least) "the great" Zig Ziglar. Although I have never met most of these people, their words and teachings have helped me mold my life in such a way that I know I am not part of the problem ... I am part of the solution!

This book is also dedicated to the Distinguished Fellowmen of Groove Phi Groove Social Fellowship Inc.®

And also, to the Mighty Brethren of Stone Square Lodge #38 F&A.M.- P.H.A. (These two great organizations took a good man and made him a better one!)

A special mention goes out to Toastmasters International and especially the members of the Woodbridge Toastmasters in Woodbridge, NJ.

Thank you for helping hone my skill and master my voice.

# WARNING:

This book is for those who are looking
to commit to making themselves better *now*.

Even though you are holding yourself
accountable
to no one other than yourself
by doing so, keep in mind that
*the universe is watching*
*and you shall be rewarded accordingly.*

If you are of the belief that your future begins
today and you are committed to making
every day better than the last by making little
changes within yourself, then take
the following pledge and put your name to it.

# PLEDGE OF ALLEGIANCE

(Write your name here)

I, _____, pledge
allegiance to my dreams in that they will
become the goals that will lead me to success;
for no matter what anyone has to say, I know
in my heart of hearts and my soul of souls
that with faith in my creator and in myself I
am destined to achieve whatever I set my
mind, heart, and body to achieve.

Today's Date:

_____

# TABLE OF CONTENTS

# FOREWORD

Professionals tend to insulate themselves from lay understanding by the development of "specialized" jargon. I have read this author's work, and he has set himself apart from being just a writer. In my understanding, he is successful in such areas as sociology, psychology, criminal justice, and other disciplines allied to the public at large. I venture to say it will be several decades before the public will come across another such document that can be utilized as a tool that fits the realm of professional usefulness.

It is clearly obvious that the reader will come to know the author of this work of art as someone who has sharpened his skills in implementing his writing techniques. He is properly prepared for the "bubble busters" and others who challenge him. In order to comprehend terminology such as "bubble buster," the reader will have to embrace the written science of language used by the author throughout the order of things. I expect a great deal of noise to be made when the book is ready for the opening, and that will be an exciting experience for not only the author but the reader as well.

—Dr. Donald K. Webster, EdD.

# INTRODUCTION

As a kid I was not very popular, probably because I always had my own way of thinking. I was not quite a leader, but I was not quite a follower either. I was just always my own person. I was comfortable in my own skin, but at the same time, I just could not find my niche amongst my peers. Basically, I do not think I have ever met a person who shares my interests with the same passion I do. I have friends with whom I share common interests, but in most, if not all, of my relationships, there is a point wherein which I see a bigger picture or a different picture altogether.

Throughout my adolescent and adult life, I learned to observe others and learned through observation the kind of man I wanted to be. I am still becoming that man, and I guess I won't know if I succeeded until I die and hopefully have the opportunity to actually, as the cliché goes, "see my life flash before my eyes." Through observation I have learned to see things as they really are, yet what I have also learned is that people in the world see things as they want them to be. In time, they make things as such, sometimes for the better, sometimes not—most often not. Additionally, there are those who may see things the way they want them to be but do nothing in terms of action to make it their reality.

When I committed myself to writing this book, I honestly did not know what I was getting myself into. However, the deeper I got into the project, I realized I was becoming a stronger person along the way. I was becoming stronger because I was becoming more and more honest with myself. I came up with the title for this book by just reflecting over my life. I am in a happy place right now, and it's only getting better. The reason for this is because I spent several years getting my mind right, and then after reaping the benefits from that course of action, I found myself in a position where I was able to get my money right by taking responsibility for my past debts and educating myself toward handling what I have now so I can have more in the future.

I also realized that when it came to achieving the things most important to me, I did what was necessary to be successful. Through my observations I learned everyone else is the same way. For example, have you ever called a friend and made plans to get together later on only for your friend to say, "Call me and remind me, okay?" If getting together is important enough to you, you shouldn't need a reminder. In life, people go after what they really want.

It could be buying a new car, a pair of designer shoes, or a bigger house. It could be one's desire to become a professional athlete, singer, or actor, or even to create or acquire a multimillion dollar company. The bottom line is if the goal is important enough to you, you will *find a way to make a way*.

This book is about making your own reality. The fact you have this book in your hands right now is proof that you can take an image in your head and make it something tangible that everyone else in the world can not only hold but also benefit from. In the pages that follow, I articulate what I have observed and experienced, and I submit them to you as lessons. I submit them to you as lessons because in retrospect I learned something from all of those observations and experiences, both good and bad. Some lessons are longer than others, and a few are just short and to the point.

Although you may feel more comfortable reading from cover to cover, there is nothing to stop you from just picking a lesson at random and reading it. Although some lessons may appear to build upon previous lessons, each lesson can also stand on its individual merit. As you read, remember that these are my opinions. Just because they work for me, I do not assert all of them will work for everyone. My advice is that you read with an open mind and try them on to see if they fit. Take what works and discard what does not.

Looking back over my life, I can remember the things that mattered most in terms of how I viewed relationships and money. The reason being the first relationship I ever witnessed—like any other child—was that between my mother and father. I watched it disintegrate before my eyes, and not only was there nothing I could do about it, I was only three years old, at which age I had neither the knowledge nor experience to even think to try to do anything about it. I just knew something was wrong. Growing up, I came to realize that the most important thing I had to get together was me. I made my mistakes, but I saw the importance of learning from them.

Just about every motivational or self-improvement book I have read encourages the reader to find some kind of mentor. In fact, this book is dedicated to many of the authors of those books, who I have adopted as mentors through their works. Basically, what they tell the reader is if there is something you want to do, find someone who is already doing it and doing it well and use them as a model. When I decided to become a motivational speaker, I did just that. I sought out those speakers who most influenced me, and I did some of the things they did that worked for me. Each of us has a different path to follow. Just like snowflakes falling in winter, no two paths are the same. Because we all have free will and individual thought, even if two people are trying to do the same thing, they may not engage in the same tactics to achieve their common goal; however, both people could very well become equally successful.

In these pages, I only wish to share some ideas with you. I only want to share what has worked for me with the hopes that it may work for you. I want for this book to be the match that lights the fire under your bottom to demand more—to demand more not from the world, your job, or the people around you, but to demand more from yourself. It is my hope that this book serves as a jump-start to your soul so you can begin running toward achieving whatever you believe will make your life better. This book is mostly a testimony of my life's journeys, past and present, as well as an extended hand inviting you to get on board and pay closer attention to your own life's journey.

One of my mentors is the motivational speaker Les Brown, who often says, "You can't get out of life alive—so you might as well enjoy the ride!" This book deals mostly with my life and how the things I experienced and observed brought me to where I am and will take me to where I want to go.

Now, I am not promising you financial riches. Personally, I am comfortable but not monetarily rich, so it would be unethical for me to call myself teaching you how to attain something I have yet to attain myself. However, I am on my way to becoming financially secure, and what I am promising you is if you take the time to make the time, keep the faith, find a way to make a way, and discipline yourself to succeeding and making no excuses along the way, you will (like the rapper 50 Cent's debut CD is entitled) Get Rich or Die Trying.

Find a way to make a way. What does this mean? There comes a time in everyone's life when if having to endure struggle after struggle and setback after setback he or she reaches a moment of clarity and says, "I'm sick and tired of being sick and tired, and I have had enough." But just acknowledging you are dissatisfied about whatever your present situation may be does not make it better. It's a start because you are acknowledging that things need to change.

Like an addict who cannot really find his or her way to sobriety until he or she admits within themselves that they are addicted, you cannot find your way to brighter days until you first admit there is a dark cloud over your head. How important to you is finding a brighter day in your life? Do you really have to reach rock bottom in order to come to the realization that things in your life need to change? Some people do. If you are reading this, hopefully you haven't reached rock bottom, but if you are there, I want you to keep the faith. It took some period of time for you to be where you are today, and it is going to take another period of time in order for you to get to where you want to be. However, if you're not happy with your life, that's a problem. No one other than you is responsible for making it better. Therefore, you're either part of the problem, or you're part of the solution.

*When you reach the end of your rope, tie a knot in it and hang on.*
*—President Franklin D. Roosevelt*

Talk is easy—and cheap; however, what makes it difficult is when you say you can and when you say you will do something, you are making affirmations to yourself that, if you are a person of integrity, you have to commit and live up to. The words commitment and integrity will be repeated countless times throughout this book.

Commitment means the act of binding yourself (intellectually or emotionally) to a course of action. Integrity means adherence to moral and ethical principles, soundness of moral character, honesty. In order for you to be able to successfully find a way to make a way to overcome the obstacles you will face on your journey, you will have to bind yourself to your course of action, and you will have to be honest and true to yourself and to those around you.

Now, when I say you have to bind yourself to your course of action that is not an absolute. There will come times when you will have to change your approach. What you are in fact binding yourself to is the act of doing something over doing nothing. Integrity comes into play because you have to be honest with yourself when something isn't working, and whichever change in course you decide to take, you must be honorable in those actions as well.

*I do not choose to be a common man; it is my right to be uncommon if I can.*

*I seek opportunity, not security. I do not wish to be a kept citizen, humbled and dulled by having the state look after me. I want to take the calculated risk, to dream and to build, to fail and to succeed.*

*I refuse to barter incentive for a dole. I prefer the challenges of life to a guaranteed existence, the thrill of fulfillment to the stale calm of Utopia. I will not trade freedom for beneficence, nor dignity for a handout.*

*It is my heritage to think and to act for myself, to enjoy the benefits of my creations, and to face the world boldly and say:*

*With God's help, this I have done.*

*Franklin D. Roosevelt*

# SECTION ONE:
# GET READY...

## Lesson One: Why Are You Here?

*Just as ships are built to sail the seas, planes to fly the heavens, and house for living, so is man created for a purpose. —Zig Ziglar*

Why are you here? As I ask you this question, I am not referring to why you are sitting in that chair. What I am asking is, **what is your purpose?** You were brought here for a reason, and by "here" I mean into this world. Every life has a purpose—every life. Those who are most successful are those who determined what their purpose was and ventured out to manifest it into reality. I guarantee that whatever it is you are doing in your life, you are capable of doing more, and when you realize for yourself that you can do more—and you actually decide to do more—in time you will see you will also have more and be more.

Don't believe me? Well, look at it like this: how many of you are married? For those of you who are, you were not born married, right? You see, at some point in your life, you decided you wanted to have more in life than casual dating relationships. For the men, when you felt you found the right woman, you dropped down on bended knee and proposed. For the women, when you "convinced" your men that you were the right woman, you also "convinced" him it would be in his best interest to drop down on bended knee (smile). Seriously, either way, a proposal was made and accepted. Perhaps sometime after the wedding—maybe one year or even five years afterwards, you decided to have a child.

Well, guess what? When that child breathes his or her first little breath, you both have more and have become more. By proposing and accepting said proposal, you have done more—more than a single person has done, and as a result, by exchanging vows before God and the world, you have gained more. You have gained a partner to stand by your side for the rest of your life. But why are you here? You see, you were once that little miracle born to your parents, and the fact that you are here today, alive, means you were guarded well. But now you're an adult. Are you doing what you always wanted to do? If so, good for you; however, even so, is there some way you could be doing it even better? If you're not doing what you want to be doing, what do you have to do in order to do what it is you want to do?

You see, this is the cause for the question why are you here? What is your mission in life? What were you destined to do? You see, if you believe in God and you believe God is all-knowing, then surely you believe he already knows, and it's you who has to figure it out. I know I had to figure it out. Every day I am still trying to figure it out. When I was in my late teens/early twenties, I spent one and a half years of my time and my father's money going to college before I realized I really did not want to be there. As a matter of fact, when I made the decision to leave school and join the U.S. Air Force that was the exact reason I gave him.

When I returned home, I realized I wanted to become a police officer because I saw there were and are people out here in the world who need help and protection, and back in the early nineties, law enforcement was taking a beating. Between all kinds of brutality allegations and cases of corruption, the cops were looking more crooked than the crooks. So, I said to myself, "If I get on the job, then I'll be taking up the spot that could have gone to someone else who wouldn't have deserved it." I don't just enjoy what I do—I have good days and bad days just like you, but I love what I do!

However, even though quite happy in my chosen career, after about my fourth year on the job, I began to feel the eerie chill of complacency creeping up on me. I have found myself asking myself, "Well, you've achieved your goals. What'cha gonna do now?" The sad part was I could not come up with an answer (and you have no idea how annoying I can be when I don't answer my own questions). In the end, I told myself I would know when God was ready for me to know.

Have any of you ever felt that way? Is that how you feel every time I ask you why are you here? Well, I understand. I understand there is struggle, but there are two important things you must understand:

1. God will not put upon you any more than you can bear.

2. God helps those who help themselves.

I have had days where I had to flip all of my couch cushions just to find change to take the bus to work, hoping I would be able to bum a ride home or otherwise face a long walk. I have had weeks that were so tight that grocery shopping for me was taking advantage of the "3 for $1" sale on Ramen noodles (hey ... with the right seasoning and some hot sauce— you don't know what you're missing). I have had to endure many a humble feast; however, all throughout those times I kept the faith that there was more in store for me. I kept the faith in that the harder I worked toward achieving my goals and the harder the journey got, the sweeter my life would turn out to be. And sweeter it has indeed become because I figured out what it was I wanted to do not once but twice!

Each and every one of us was delivered onto this earth with some kind of divine purpose. However, we were also delivered here with free will. Sadly, many people live their lives and go to their graves without ever discovering their purpose. On the flip side, many people go through various trials and tribulations until they find themselves in a position where there is nothing left for them to do but serve as an example of what not do, as is the case with people who may have lived lives of crime but upon finding themselves incarcerated realize the best thing for them to do is steer at-risk youth away from the same fate that befell them.

I decided a long time ago that I wanted my life to mean something—that when my time comes to "go home," I will have left a positive mark on someone's life. As such, I decided to steer my life's direction toward service. Being a firm believer in karma—the concept that what you put out into the world you get back in return—I cannot, in good conscience, talk to you about getting what you want in life without also speaking about service. There is scripture that tells us, "To whom much is given, much is required." You see, that's a universal standard.

In order to receive God's blessings, you must first yourself become a blessing. When I was nineteen, I decided I did not want to be in college, but I wanted whatever I did with my life at that time to have some kind of purpose. I left college and joined the U.S. Air Force in order to serve my country. When I came back after Desert Storm, I went back to school, pledged, and became a distinguished fellowman of Groove Phi Groove Social Fellowship Incorporated®, and to this day (nearly twenty years later), I remain a dedicated member because we act to serve the community, and I later became a police officer so that I may serve society.

In 2006, I came to the decision that I wanted to become a motivational speaker. I feel that I have something to say and something to give, and I want to share it with the world. If you are reading this book, then you are at the right place at the right time.

By reading this book, you might be in a place in your life where you're uncertain of what your purpose may be, and you are searching for it, and that's okay! That's not a good thing; that's a great thing! As you search for your purpose, however, do not just try to formulate something that only you benefit from. If you deem your purpose in life to do whatever you think will benefit only you, trust me when I tell you that in the end you will come up short and find yourself lacking. I do not believe I shall be rewarded in return for what I do. I believe I shall be rewarded for what I do for others. That is why I am here. Ask yourself ... why are you here?

*The best way to determine what your life's purpose should be now is to determine what you want people to say about you at your funeral and then live up to it until that day comes.*
*—HSRjr*

## Lesson Two: Life Gives You What You Ask of It

*Your success will be in direct proportion to the quality and quantity of ideas that you can generate to improve your current circumstances. —Brian Tracy*

What do you want to have? What and who do you want to be? What do you deserve?

Everyone knows about the genie in the magic lamp. You rub the lamp, and when the genie comes out in a big plume of smoke, he offers you three wishes. So, what do you wish for? You have three opportunities to gain whatever it is you desire. Do you wish for a million dollars? Well, in this day and age, it's a good start but is not much money on a global scale. So, do you wish for a "ga-trillion" dollars? Do you wish for world peace? Do you wish to not have to pay taxes ... ever? You've got three wishes! So, let's say you go the money route and get the "ga-trillion" dollars ... poof ... wish number one. Now, you want your children to grow up in a safe world, so you wish for world peace ... poof ... wish number two. Now, you have one last wish.

What do you wish for? Decisions ... decisions! You are rich and the world is at peace—what more could you possibly want? How about a beautiful actor/actress, model, or singer waiting for you at home in a French-maid outfit (for the men) or some Speedos (for the ladies)? Poof! The men come home to find a beautiful woman, and the ladies come home to find the man of their dreams, and life is good. I have only one question for you now that you have used up all of your wishes—what if your first wish was to wish for more than three wishes?

What if you told the genie, "For my first wish, I want three extra wishes for every wish I make"? What about a cure for AIDS, cancer, herpes, or even the common cold? There are people—children, who are homeless and starving in Africa, the Middle East, Little Rock, Brooklyn, Newark, and probably within a one-hundred-mile radius of where you live. Imagine how much more good you could have done instantly by wishing for more wishes. Imagine if, for every wish you made, you received three more.

Your ability to do good would compound with every wish, and all you had to do to receive that ability was ask for it. I hope none of you reading this ever experiences the danger and the violation of being robbed, but as a matter of practice, thieves often work by one of two modus operandi (or both):

1. "Give me everything you got," which is self-explanatory.

2. "What else ya got?" This is when, after you have given up your money, they then demand your jewelry and whatever else you have. (As a police officer, I have known people lucky enough to leave such encounters in possession of only their underwear and their lives.)

Naturally, I am by no means endorsing any kind of illegal activity; however, criminals as described in the above example don't just demand one item from their victims. They either demand everything up front or they keep demanding. On a more positive note, let's say your best friend comes to you and says, "Over the years, you've been by my side through thick and thin. I just came into a ton of money, and I'm going to share it with you. How much do you want?" How much are you going to ask for? Who is going to determine the extent of your friend's generosity, you or him/her? So, you say, "Well, I could use about two hundred dollars," and your friend gives you $200 cash. But then your friend says, "I just inherited over a million dollars. I would have given you twenty thousand dollars!"

What if you had a job offer and the potential employer told you to determine your starting salary? Would you ask for a couple hundred dollars more than your present salary? Would you ask for a couple thousand more? How about ten thousand more? What if you asked for the ten thousand-dollar raise and actually got it? You see, life works in a similar fashion. If you do not want anything out of life, then life will ensure you do not get anything.

If you try to be too humble and ask for far less than what you want or feel you are worth, you will get what you asked for … and not what you wanted. On the flip side, if you want that high-paying salary or that executive position or that attractive man or woman you see every day on the train, at some point you are going to have to step up and stake your claim. In the mid-1800s, over a quarter of a million people migrated to various parts of the California desert in search of gold.

They would declare a patch of land, register their declaration with the government, and thus have full ownership of whatever they produced on that land. Some people made fortunes; some did not. What is important here is that those who made their fortunes did so because they ventured out and staked their claim.

Now granted, you can ask God for anything you want. You could have every justification in the world explaining why you should have that job. However, if all you're going to do is ask, don't expect opportunity to come knocking at your door anytime soon. You see, wanting alone is not enough. Earlier when we were talking about the genie and the magic lamp, we were talking about wishing.

Wishing is wanting more out of life without wanting to work for it, and those who want more without wanting to work for it will always be looking for that genie. The funny thing is that today people are not rubbing on lamps. They are rubbing off scratch-off lottery cards and are dumping hundreds to thousands of dollars a year—all believing that lottery sales pitch, "All it takes is a dollar and a dream," or the other one, "You've got to be in it to win it."

Personally, I like that last one, "You've got to be in it to win it." I just do not believe that throwing away my hard-earned money on six random numbers is a productive or even smart way to become financially free, or to at least just get ahead of my bills. The "it" that I want to be in to win is the game of life. The game of life is the one game you cannot get out of alive, so... "You've got to be in it to win it!"

I have a confession to make. When I first released this book, I did it on my own, as I had not yet met signed a deal with a publishing house. I paid a company to take my manuscript and convert it from a Word document into book form. I had taken my ideas, put them into words, put them on paper, and actually produced a book. Unfortunately, by going the self-publishing/print-on-demand route, I didn't have the marketing and promotional resources that a publishing house has, so I was selling books any and everywhere I could. Between September of 2007 and the spring of 2008, I bought two hundred copies. I kept a box in my trunk, and if I had a speaking engagement, I would have a table in the back of the room, and after my speech I would be selling and signing books.

I received support (and sales) from friends all over. I opened a PayPal account and sold books online. I remember one occasion when I shared a table with my wife, Taria, who was displaying her photography at a street fair. People would walk by and look at her work and then look at my book. Because Taria took the photo used for the cover, we had a huge poster-sized copy made, which we framed and sat upon an easel.

My friend Rich would walk up and down the street with a copy of the book in his hand and tell people where I was and that I was signing books there. The people walking by would be shocked to actually see the guy in the poster and on those books standing right in front of them. After some small talk, some people congratulated me, thanked me for the conversation, and walked on to the other tables.

Although not every person bought a copy that day, there was not one single person that walked up, looked around, and walked away without me or my friend Rich working to put a book in their hand. Every single person was more than a friendly conversation— they were also a potential sale.

Many of those sales came from me coming flat out and saying, "The book is only $19.99. How about I sign a copy for you right now? When I'm on Oprah, you can show your friends your personally autographed copy!" I got those sales because I asked for them. I even sold a copy to my mayor that day! So, what do you want out of life? You have to know. If you don't figure it out for yourself, then life will figure it out for you, and you might not care for what you get.

Think of yourself as a vessel out to sea. Now, either you can be like a rowboat with no oars or a rudder, subject to wherever the tide takes you, or you can have a vision or goal for yourself in mind as your destination and have your expressed desire aligned with your active efforts act as your oars and rudder, with which you will have the ability to steer yourself in the direction you want to go.

Just like a department store or supermarket, the universe exists to give us what we want; however, just like those places, you can't just walk up and take it off the shelf. What you can do, though, is ask the "sales associate" (God, family, and friends) for help in making sure you get the right item in the right size!

I can honestly say that just about everything in life I ever truly wanted I have gotten, and the same can apply to you. What you have to realize—and I cannot repeat this enough times—people won't know what you want if you never ask for it, and although God does know what you want, if you're not going to be brave enough to claim it, he will allow you to watch someone else, someone who was brave enough to stake their claim, reap the rewards of your dreams.

# <u>*Lesson Three: Nothing Worth Having Comes Easy*</u>

*Those heights by great men, won and kept, were not achieved by sudden flight. But they, while their companions slept, toiled upward in the night.*
*—Henry Wadsworth Longfellow*

*He who knows no hardship will know no hardihood. He who faces no calamity will need no courage. Mysterious though it is, the characteristics in human nature we love best grow in a soil with a strong mixture of troubles.*
*—Harry Emerson Fosdick*

Life is about balance. You have to take the bad with the good and the bitter with the sweet. If every day were sunny, how could you appreciate it? There is no such thing as perfection; it's an illusion. In life, you need to have some adversity in order to excel. To be perfect means there is no room for improvement, and who do any of us know who cannot afford to improve in one area or another? My cousin Paula and her (genius of a) son, Darryl, ripped this book apart in proofreading it … and I found I still had more corrections to make!

You can have what you want in life, but if it is something that bears significant enough meaning to you, you're going to have to endure some form of struggle and/or sacrifice in order to prove yourself worthy and deserving in the eyes of the universe. Sometimes it may be a matter of effort; in other words, just getting up off of your bottom and putting in some good old-fashioned elbow grease.

Other times it may just be a matter of timing; in other words, the timing might not be right, and you'll have to be patient while riding out the storm. I can think of many times where I had to endure the struggles of getting something—or even someone—I may have wanted, but I think the first time I ever had to just wait because there was nothing else for me to do was when I was about maybe ten or eleven years old. I had a really bad spill on my bicycle, which damaged the fork holding the front wheel intact. I had to wait, I think, six weeks for it to come in.

*Patience can't be acquired overnight. It is just like building up a muscle. Every day you need to work on it. —Eknath Easwaran*

Every day indeed was spent working on building up my patience. Day after day it just seemed like getting that bicycle part was going to take forever. In fact, day after day my bicycle part was one day closer to coming to me. When it finally did come, it was like all the waiting was worth it.

There will be times in life when you'll have to just wait until you are ready and in the right position to do what it is you want to do or have what it is you want to have. In this case it's not enough to just be patient; you have to be doing something. Being patient does not just mean sitting on your duff waiting for what you want to happen like I had to do with the bicycle part. You may have to spend that time building yourself up to be ready to handle what it is you want to have or be. When I was in grade school, my father was not one to buy me all of the name-brand sneakers and jeans that some of my friends' parents bought them.

His reasoning was, "I'm not spending my good money on something that you're going to just tear up in a couple of weeks." For about four or five years, my shoes and sneakers came from some no-name store where you could buy one pair of shoes at regular price and get another at half price. When they had sales, you could get the second pair for a dollar. In my mind, my father was just being cheap. He did not have to experience the ridicule I went through on a nearly daily basis when the other kids at school would "crack" on (make fun of) my occasional "high water" pants or my no-name shoes. My only support from him in that area was, "If they don't like your clothes, let them buy you some new ones."

As the years passed and I became old enough and able enough to afford some of those fancy things, I learned to appreciate them more because I bought them with my own money. Even if my father saw some of the things I bought as a waste, it really did not matter because it was my money to waste. However, and this is the point, when I came across those things I wanted that I knew my father was not going to buy for me, if I really wanted it, I found a way to make a way to get them, and the truth is, in the long run, some of those things I bought really were a waste of money!

Nonetheless, I can still say that just about everything I ever wanted I got, and I carried that lesson into adulthood— not just with regard to buying things, but also with regard to becoming the man I am today. I am married to a beautiful woman. I met my wife, Taria (pronounced like "Maria"), when I had close to nothing. When I met her, I was already on the path of patience in that I had set my goal to become a police officer.

In pursuit of this goal, I was basically in that position where all I could do was wait for it to come to me and keep the hope alive. I was a loss prevention agent for Old Navy, barely making $21,000 a year, and I was still living under my father's roof in East Orange, New Jersey. She and I had been dating for about maybe three weeks before I met her parents, and I remember the first time I went to her house to meet them. She lived in a big house near the end of a cul-de-sac filled with other big houses in Monroe, New Jersey. When I pulled up to the house, I have to admit I was taken aback. I thought to myself, "Her family is loaded!"

Then I began wondering if her parents would look down on me because I was from East Orange, a city that's just a wee bit more "hood" than Monroe, which is to politely say Monroe is not "hood" at all. Nonetheless, I took a deep breath and rang the doorbell. After meeting her family, Taria began to give me a tour of the house. The best part of the tour was when she took me downstairs into the basement. This was her father's space, decked out just for him by him. When you went downstairs you entered his "office," where he had his desk and computer all set up and running.

The office led into another room with a huge couch against one wall and a very impressive entertainment system against the other. There was a large-screen television and two large speakers on both sides of the couch and the television. Taria told me that her father used to have a little disc jockey business years back, and that's where all of the sound equipment came from. In a house full of women, this was "man's space!" I said to Taria (and to myself), "When I get my own place, I want to have a room just like this!"

A few months before we got married, we moved into our first apartment, which came with a huge basement, and although it never quite got as decked out as her father's basement, it was mine, and I made into my own "man's space!" When we moved in, I remember telling her, "I don't care what you do upstairs, but the basement is mine!" It would be about another three years from that day before we moved into our first apartment. At the time I was still living at home with my father—and even in my own apartment, but my apartment was still in his house.

It was about a year and a half into our relationship that I "popped the big question." I had known long before that I did not want to raise my family in an inner-city environment, yet at the same time, I knew I did not want to live too far away from work. So, in addition to planning our wedding, Taria and I were trying to figure out where we were going to live with the hopes of our home being someplace in between where our parents lived. During the time we were in the wedding planning stages, I was offered a job via "lateral transfer" with the agency I now work for.

The only requirement imposed upon me was that I would have to be a resident of the township by the time I was set to be hired some three months away. Considering the fact that Woodbridge Township was pretty much in the middle of where our parents lived, as well as the significant raise in pay I was in line to receive, there really was not much discussion necessary concerning where we were going to live. Now again, the message of this lesson is nothing worth having comes easy, and here too is where it applies. In my father's house I paid $400 a month for what would cost an average renter maybe $900 to $1,000 a month.

The only problem was the fact that my father's house was just that—my father's house. It was not mine, and as such, I was pretty much subject to his will. What he wanted was what he got. Even though the opportunity was there to live there even after getting married and still pay less than the average renter would, that was not an option, and plus with the new job offer, the situation pretty much settled itself. So, what wound up happening was Taria and I moved into our first little apartment together about three months before our wedding. The rent was around $975 a month, more than twice what I was paying in the comfort of my father's house, but even though I was paying more, it was mine (and I got my "man's space" down in the basement).

The first time my father came to visit us, before Taria served us lunch, I was downstairs, and he sat at the head of my table. Taria respectfully suggested that he choose another chair, as the chair he was in was mine, but he sort of brushed her off. When I came upstairs and asked him to move, before he could brush me off, my cousin Gene—who came with my father— reminded him, "You're in his house now." When my father stood up and moved to another seat, it felt good. At that point, all of the extra money I was paying in rent and utilities was well worth it. Now, with the new job offer on the horizon, I was feeling really good.

I felt good all the way up until I was informed by my current job at the time that they were not going to allow me to take the other job. You see, there were all kinds of State Department of Personnel Civil Service requirements that had to be met in order for the transfer to go through, and the hitch came in where even though the offer was made by one agency, my current one had to agree on the transfer also—and they did not. So, there I was, disgusted, but I understood why things had transpired, and because I understood why, I was able to formulate how I would see my way through. You see, I knew that civic relations were all messed up in my hometown.

The mayor did not get along with the police chief, and the police officers, for the most part, did not get along with one another. Everyone felt they deserved to be paid more (they did—and still do), and there had not been a new contract (or raises) in over three years. I was not the only officer looking for new opportunities elsewhere, nor was I the only officer whose efforts to go elsewhere were shot down. Yet, I saw the bigger picture, which was quite simple. "What we do for you we have to do for everyone else," and with that mentality, had the brass allowed me or any other officer to take advantage of a lateral transfer offer, the door would have to be open for everyone to do so. I truly believe were that to happen "doors" would not be open—floodgates would be opened, and there would have been a mass exodus. So, I accepted my situation for what it was—an obstacle.

I sent a letter to the chief and deputy chief of police at the offering agency, and I informed them that my request to accept their job offer had been rejected by my superiors. I remember telling them that I could have looked at the situation one of two different ways: one, as if my superiors were purposely trying to hold me down and keep me from bettering myself away from them (which I still think is very much true); and the other, I had such potential and promise that they did not want to lose a patrolman like me (not as likely as the first possibility— but I believe there was some truth in that one as well).

In any case, I told them I was going to take the high road and believe that my current agency just didn't want to lose me, but I also told them not to forget my name, for they would be hearing from me again. You see, sometimes you just have to let time do its thing. The saying "time heals all wounds" is very much true. I could have been bitter like just about everyone else I was working with. In all levels of my current agency at the time, they had their reasons for their bitterness, and now I had mine, but I opted not to let the situation beat me down. I turned inward and upward for patience and strength.

I focused on continuing to do good work, and a year later a new civil service exam came around. I took the test and passed the test. By that time, I was already living in Woodbridge, and adding my veteran's preference to the fact the residency requirement was no longer an issue, that's where my scores went to first. I'll admit, I did not pass with a stellar score, but being a veteran and entitled to veterans' preference, my placing shot up to number three on the township's hiring list. On the afternoon of November 25, 2002, I received a phone call from the Woodbridge Police Department telling me that everything had gone through successfully, and I was hired.

When I got off the phone, I typed up several copies of my resignation letter to disperse to the various links in my chain of command, and when I went to work that evening, disperse them is exactly what I did. When I went to the new personnel office to sign my hiring and tax forms, I expected to be told that my salary was going to be what was offered to me when I first met with the chief the previous year; however, to my surprise, I was told that my time already on the job, albeit as short as it was, had been taken into consideration, and the chief of police had decided to pay me at the next pay grade above what I had originally been offered.

This came out to be just under $10,000 more than that original offer and just over $17,000 more than I was already making. I left my former agency and entered a new agency making just about as much, if not a little bit more, than my former sergeant made. With raises and contracts being settled in reasonable periods of time, after four years, in 2006, I made $105,000. My salary as a patrolman had become more than likely equivalent to what my former lieutenants' salaries were. I haven't made less than $100,000 a year ever since. During the course of those four years, I was able to move into a bigger apartment so that my then newborn son (A.J.) could have his own room; I was able to climb out of some pretty deep debt, and in the summer of 2006, I bought my first home.

Now, these were by no means easy tasks to accomplish, but had I not opted to step out of my comfort zone and stay focused on the bigger picture— my goal to improve myself, both professionally and financially—I probably would have wound up still in that low-paying job, and I probably would be as bitter as my former coworkers. Now granted, I have bitter coworkers with the agency I work for now but coming from where I came from and enduring the things I had to endure to get to where I am, I see things from a perspective I don't think they could ever understand. My trials and tribulations have brought me to a place of appreciation for a lot of the things some of my present coworkers take for granted.

*Do your work. Not just your work, but a little bit more for the lavishing sake. And if you suffer, as you will, do your work. And out of your work and suffering will come the great joys of life.*
*—LeBaron Russell Briggs, Dean—Harvard University*

As I have said before and will more than likely say again, just wanting something does not entitle you to have it. If it is significant enough and if it is meant to be yours, the universe will put you to the test to see if you are worthy of what it is you want. Oftentimes you have more appreciation for something you had to struggle to attain as opposed to something just given to you. This works in all aspects of life: work, money, sports, relationships, etc. It took nearly ten years for me to become a police officer, so I appreciate my career because of all of the obstacles I had to overcome and endure in order to get in it and excel within it.

The problem most people have, especially in today's society, is that they want everything now. It used to take days to send someone a message. Today you can log on and share "instant" messages with a person on the other side of the planet. Years ago, you had to buy coffee beans from the store, grind them, and filter water through them in order to get a cup of coffee. Today the shelves in the market are stocked with "instant" coffee. It used to take about fifteen to twenty minutes to make popcorn, but today you put the bag in the microwave, push the preprogrammed "popcorn" button, and in two to three minutes you've got a hot bag of fluffy popcorn—with butter!

The end result: more ease in consumption; however, on a far larger scale, the results have proven to be far more detrimental. Because of all of our technological advances over the decades, people have contracted an anaphylactic response to labor. In other words, they have become allergic to work. There used to be a time when adulthood came early because every able body was needed in order to work and support the family unit.

Children learned early the value of a hard day's work, and that was carried along with them into adulthood. However, at some point in time—perhaps somewhere in the transition between the agricultural, industrial, and information ages—the idea of the American dream being something earned became an idea where people began believing it is something they were entitled to. I believe it is because of this that many immigrants have been able to come to this country virtually penniless and within a decade become practically financially independent while millions of people who are born and raised here do so little with what they have.

Those who have the American dream but do nothing toward making that dream come true are still just dreaming. In my twenties, before becoming a police officer, I worked for a few security companies. I was one of those flashlight-carrying drones that people insultingly call "rent-a-cops," but let me tell you something, it was one of the most humbling and educational experiences of my life. I really hated those jobs, but I saw myself as being "on the grind" and gaining experience for a career in law enforcement. What I came to learn was that none of those jobs prepared me for my career in law enforcement. None of those companies cared about grooming their employees for corporate growth. All those companies care about is keeping the money coming in by keeping their clients satisfied, and to do that they needed bodies to fill slots and be present at the assigned sites.

Because I hated those jobs, I would go to work and then go home. However, there were times when I would have to stay an hour or so later if my relief was late or until they found a replacement. I cannot tell you how many men and women I met who were immigrants and would jump at any and every opportunity to make that overtime money. What I took for granted they just took! Now, I do not know if any of them ever became rich, but what I did learn from that experience was that those people came here to this country to work. The $8 an hour that I just knew wasn't what I was worth was practically a fortune compared to what those people would have been making in their home countries.

In time, I learned the only thing this world owes any of us is a place to live and a place to die. Everything that goes on in between is entirely up to us. Life does not give you what you ask of it just because you want it. Life gives you what you ask of it when you have proven yourself deserving of it. This is why it is very rare that you will encounter a generous friend willing to just give you $20,000. This is why you won't just go home and find the man or woman of your dreams just waiting to fulfill your every desire, and certainly why you will more than likely never find that magic lamp with the genie inside!

The reason nothing worth having comes easy is because you have to be made to appreciate the things you say matter most to you. That appreciation is forged in the trials and tribulations you endure on the way to achieving your goals. You never know when the universe will open up and say, "You've had enough; you are worthy." If you just give in halfway through the struggle, two things happen: one, it becomes harder for you to endure future struggles (and there will be future struggles); and two, it becomes easier to walk away and quit when the road gets bumpy.

You could be at the very brink of success and not know it—especially if you quit and give up the struggle. I remember in 1999 when I had reached my wit's end trying to become a police officer. I was getting rejected by agencies out of state, and my hometown agency had strung me along for about a year only to let me down. I had a good job and a decent future at Old Navy, plus the parent company, Gap Inc., offered a tuition reimbursement program, so I decided to return to school in the spring semester, which began in January of 2000. On the first day of school, I went to my scheduled classes and received my syllabuses. When I got home at the end of the day, there was a letter from the East Orange Police Department informing me I was officially hired and would be starting at the police academy that following February.

*We are so often caught up in our destination that we forget to appreciate the journey, especially the goodness of the people we meet on the way. Appreciation is a wonderful feeling, don't overlook it. —Unknown*

You have to push on. Nothing worth having comes easily. If it did, how could you appreciate it? Let us revisit the scenario where your best friend offered to share his financial windfall with you. Never mind how he got the money; what matters here is that you were given the money. Sure, you "earned" it by being a loyal friend; however, if in being a friend your goal was to someday receive some kind of financial gain, you really need to look up the words "loyalty" and "friendship" in the dictionary. In this scenario, you were given the money, and chances are likely you will spend that money.

First, you will probably catch up on some bills, maybe even pay a little extra just to get ahead. Next, you might put a few dollars in your savings account, but after that … it's party time! And a while after that, the money is gone—and your bills are there waiting for you with a smile and an open hand. Now, had you personally worked for and earned that money on your own, chances are you might not be so eager to spend it so freely and easily. Going back to those who play the lottery, statistically, the majority of those who do win find themselves right back where they started before they won and in only a matter of a few years.

Looking back, I realized that this is what I learned from my father's "frugality," and I too have become just as "frugal." The fact of the matter is I come from a long line of "frugal" men! Again, nothing worth having comes easily. To this day, I consider myself one of the luckiest people in the universe because, for all intents and purposes, I had indeed quit. I found the following poem shortly afterwards and have lived by it ever since:

*When things go wrong as they sometimes will. When the road you're trudging seems all up hill. When funds are low and the debts are high. And you want to smile, but you have to sigh. When care is pressing you down a bit. Rest, if you must, but don't you quit. Life is queer with its twists and turns. As every one of us sometimes learns. And many a failure turns about. When he might have won had he stuck it out: Don't give up though the pace seems slow, you may succeed with another blow. Success is failure turned inside out – The silver tint of the clouds of doubt. And you never can tell how close you are. It may be near when it seems so far. So stick to the fight when you're hardest hit – It's when things seem worst that you must not quit. — Unknown*

## Lesson Four: Beware Of The Bubble Busters!

### *The optimist takes action—the pessimist takes a seat. —Zig Ziglar*

**Disclaimer:** *This particular piece pertains to everyone reading it. Just like the game of life, there's a part for everyone to play. When you read this, you will know which part is yours because it will be who you are that picks the part for you. If the part you play empowers you—great! If the part you play offends you—I may have struck a nerve, but as long as you are blessed enough to wake up, you've got more than enough time to make a change.*

This lesson may very well prove to be one of the most important lessons in this entire book. Although I firmly believe we are responsible for our own individual destinies, it is also equally true that one person people fail to blame for their shortcomings is themselves. People are more inclined to blame someone else for their setbacks and mistakes. Granted, there are people who are born under lucky stars where they may have little to no worries, but then again, there are those who came from little or nothing and worked themselves up to being successful and happy with their personal and professional lives.

At the same time, these are people that many silently or blatantly despise because they themselves aren't living the lifestyles they see in the magazines and on television. People see the fancy clothes, cars, and homes and, despite wishing they could have those very things, denigrate the people who have them. The fact of the matter is this: if you're reading this book, then you are one of the select few seeking membership into an incredibly exclusive fraternity. This fraternity has no name, but its purpose is simple: the attainment of success. Success in life, in love, in work, in whatever you deem important.

You want, and even better, know that someday you're going to be at the top. When you came to the decision that you were going to commit yourself to succeeding, you may have felt a tingling in your belly. I know when I made that decision I had some things going on inside me. I sincerely hope that by the time you finish reading this book that tingling sensation inside of you will have transformed into at least a spark, or at best a flame, to drive you on to the next experience in your journey. The funny thing is that when that tingling sensation evolves into a spark, that's when the ideas start running wild in your mind. You start thinking about what it is you want to do. You begin asking yourself, "What's my thing going to be?" and in that excitement you go out and share your vision with a friend and/or relative.

However, have you ever shared your goals, plans, or hopes with someone only to have them tell you why you couldn't do what you wanted to set out to do? Aren't these the same people who say, "I'm only telling you this for your own good so you don't waste your time chasing empty dreams"? Aren't these the same people who spend more time telling you what you are incapable of doing as opposed to opening their minds to try to see things through your eyes? There is a name I have given these people. These people are the "bubble busters," and they live to do just that—bust your bubble! These are the people who, when you tell them you want to start your own business, say, "What do you know about doing 'so and so'? What happens if no one buys your product? You'll lose everything. You better stay where you are." I want you to believe in the greatness that exists within you. Trust me when I tell you that it's there!

There is physical greatness, and then there is mental greatness. Not that you need a lesson in the birds and the bees, but you know that when two people lay down and set out to create life, a portion of one is mixed with a portion of the other, conception occurs, and the miracle of life begins. Unless you cheat and get a sonogram, you won't know if you've made a boy or a girl, but you know you're going to get one or the other … unless you have twins! No matter what, a beautiful bundle of physical greatness is coming your way in nine months, and where did it come from? He or she came from within you!

Have you ever said something that made another person smile when they were feeling low? Have you ever found yourself in a pickle of a predicament and then find your way out of it? Have you ever gotten an A on a test or even a hard-earned B? Do you have an idea of what you may want to do with your life? If not, and you believe you need to get an idea, all of these things are just very small examples of your mental greatness! In short, the body will achieve just about whatever the mind believes. (No, it won't! That doesn't apply to everybody!) There go those bubble busters—look out!

These are the people who know what they know, and many of them might even go so far as to tell you they know you better than you know yourself. Don't listen to them! It's bad enough that the majority of your inner dialogue is negative; you don't need somebody else agreeing with it. Now, before I go on any further, not every person who tells you that you are incapable of doing something is a bubble buster. Although there is greatness within you all, that does not mean you are destined to be great at everything you set out to do.

Sometimes someone might actually be telling you what you need to hear as opposed to what you want to hear. You have to be honest with yourself. If you feel there is a competitive body builder inside of you, but you've got "belly-do," then you might want to reconsider your options. Oh, you don't know what "belly-do" is? That's when your muscles don't stick out as much as your "belly do."

However, if you are willing to put forth the work necessary to bring that body builder out, then go for it! Seriously, look at the people on American Idol. Tell the truth—don't most of us watch the first two weeks when they have on the most horrible singers to ever open their mouths? I'm not a mean person, and I'm sure most of you aren't either, but come on—when someone stands in front of you and sounds like a moose in heat, none of us could be guilty of being called bubble busters if we advised that person to stick to his or her day job.

You see, there is a difference between someone who is being a pessimist and someone who is being a realist. If you were told by everyone around you there was no way you could ever become a scientist even though you got straight A's in the subject throughout your entire scholastic career and you wound up doing something else other than what you obviously excelled in, then you were totally surrounded by pessimistic people who you allowed to poison your mind. However, if you got it in your head that you wanted to become a bio-nuclear physicist after seeing some kind of inspiring movie but you got straight D's and F's in basic science, then those naysayers might be coming from a more realistic point of view that you should pay some attention to.

People who are happy in their own little comfort zone "hate" to see someone try to leave them in that zone. After all, misery loves company. If you're twenty-two years old and five-foot-three with no chances of growing another inch for the rest of your life, what are your chances of slam-dunking a basketball, let alone making it into the NBA? Wait a minute—Tyrone "Mugsy" Bogues was twenty-two years old when he was picked by the Washington Bullets in the 1987 NBA draft. Not only has Mugsy been known to occasionally get a dunk in, in a 1993 game against the New York Knicks, he managed to block a shot by Patrick Ewing, who just so happens to be seven feet tall!

How many bubble busters in his life do you think are eating crow now? Sometimes you just have to go for your dreams, and other times you have to be honest with yourself and know when you've reached either the apex of your ability, even if that level is not a great one, or what you set out for is just not yours. That reminds me of a song by George Clinton called "Chocolate City," in which he says, "To each his reach, and if I don't cop it ain't mine to have." Everyone is entitled to shoot for their dreams, but as I have repeatedly said, just because you want something does not necessarily mean it is guaranteed to be yours.

Basically, what that means is you just might have to find something else—and there is no shame in that. You will just have to find something that you're good at and can get even better at. You have to find what works for you; however, if it's not something you love, something that drives your passion, and you happen to excel at it, well then, you just might risk becoming a victim of your own success.

In my career as a police officer, I'm not as spitfire gung-ho as I was when I came out of the academy, but I'm nowhere near the point where I just want to coast out the rest of my days—especially since I'm just a short fifteen years away from when I plan to retire! However, a couple of years ago, I was partnered with an officer who wanted to do as little as possible. It got really tired really quick, and as much as I hated being inside, I went to my lieutenant and said, "If I can't be productive outside, I'd rather be productive inside."

He assigned me to the radio where I dispatched calls to the cops on the street, and it was a sweet gig—but after about six months, I began to notice that officers I had seniority over were getting picked over me for certain assignments. One night, when a rookie with less than a year on the street got picked over me for a particular assignment, I reached my boiling point. When I approached my lieutenant about it, he told me he needed me where I fit best—on the radio. I said, "So, basically I'm a victim of my own success?" and his answer was a soft but certain "Yes." With that, I jumped at the first opportunity to get off of that squad and get back out on the street before I found myself put out to pasture too soon. I came to find out that soon after I left the squad the officer I was originally partnered with became the radio officer.

In life, you have to find the balance between what you're good at and what you enjoy doing. The word that was created for doing something that you're good at but hate doing is work. In the beginning, I spoke of the greatness that exists within us all. Let's revisit that. You have to figure out what it is you want to do with yourself. Then you have to figure out how you're going to do it. Then you're going to have to go about doing it. In my studies, Anthony Robbins gave me what he called "The Ultimate Success Formula." First, you set the goal; second, take action toward achieving it; third, evaluate your progress; fourth, change your approach as necessary until you achieve your goal.

So, let's say you know what you want to do. Let's say it's something that is not totally out of reach for you. What do you do next? Get to work. Whatever goal you set for yourself, learn what is required of you—and then do it. When I decided I wanted to become a speaker, I began learning my craft. I began reading books, watching DVDs, and listening to learning programs all about effective speaking. I joined

Toastmasters International, which I learned of from world-famous motivational speaker Les Brown. I began to learn my craft.

Now, you've got to be very careful about whom you share your goals and dreams with because that's when the bubble busters come out. The bubble busters come into play when you get so excited about what it is you've decided to do that you want to share it with just about everyone. As a matter of fact, the inspiration for the name "bubble buster" came from a very close friend who is not typically one I would call a bubble buster but after reading one of my motivational blogs gave me a lot of negative feedback.

In all fairness to him, even though the feedback was negative, because I knew where he was coming from— and knowing it was not a place of trying to be a bubble buster, I was able to take heed to his comments and apply them to this particular lesson. In short, I was able to take his negative feedback and implement it into my program so that it became a positive for me in the end. Now, speaking of turning negatives into positives, my father is a big time bubble buster. No matter what the situation, he will be the one to tell you what could go wrong. It got to a point where I would not tell my dad about certain decisions I made or courses of action I was planning to take.

When he first read the words "my father is a big time bubble buster," I think I hurt his feelings. I really had to get him to see past that one sentence and see how he (unknowingly) taught me important lessons about doing things for myself in terms of both getting the things I wanted in life and doing the things that made me happy. If I erred, he would be the first one to tell me I should have gone to him for advice. I can still hear him telling me, "You think you know everything! You never want to hear what I have to say because you don't want to hear anything negative!" Now, I was raised to not talk back to my elders, so I never did reply, "You're right! Why would I want to hear anything negative? I can do bad all by myself!" Sure, I made mistakes, we all make mistakes on this journey we call life, but I learned from my mistakes— and you will too! Bubble busters live to remind you of your mistakes, not to get you to learn from your mistakes but to belittle you and discourage you from trying again.

So, if you ever find yourself in an encounter with someone who says to you, "Oh, you tried that before and you failed! Why do you want to try that again?" I want you to respond, "I'll tell you why ... because I want to be better than I am! Because I want to have more than I have! Because I want to do better than I am doing now!" The next time you find yourself facing a bubble buster, ask that person, "What are you doing to better yourself? Who are you to tell me what I'm incapable of doing?"

*No one on the face of this earth can make you feel inferior without your permission. —Zig Ziglar*

You see, the funny thing about bubble busters is the one bubble they cannot bust is the one they live in! They are comfortable in the bubble they live in. Bubble busters refuse to break out of their comfort zones and don't want you to break out of yours!

*Mediocre people often criticize and denigrate the successful people in their industries. They complain about them behind their backs and point out their faults and shortcomings. They get together with other average performers and gossip about the industry leaders and tell stories. These behaviors are invariably fatal to success. No one who criticizes the high performers in their industry ever becomes a high performer himself. —Brian Tracy*

You have to break out of your comfort zone in order to succeed. You cannot build your vocabulary if all you read are comic strips. You can't expect to run and complete a marathon if you can't run a mile without puking and/or passing out. You can't build up the muscles in your body if you don't exert yourself beyond the pain. Don't let the bubble busters of the world tell you what you can't do. Set your goals and your sights as high as you desire. Be realistic, but by no means be reasonable. That's right—I'm telling you to be unreasonable. Imagine the great things that exist because people chose to be unreasonable.

The world was proven to not be flat by an unreasonable man. Human flight was proven possible by unreasonable men. The belief that it was humanly impossible to run a four-minute mile was shattered by an unreasonable man. Like Les Brown says, "You can't stroll to your goal," and "You have to think of failure as part of the process and not the end of the process." With that said, so what if you stumble along the way? So, what if your first ninety-nine attempts fail? So, what if your first one hundred attempts fail? At least you dared! The greatest athletes miss more shots than they make.

What if Jordan stopped playing basketball when he missed his first shot? When he did all he could do in basketball and failed in baseball, he still walked away a successful multimillionaire, right? He took a chance, evaluated the results, and went back to what worked. You can do bad all by yourself! Don't let the bubble busters of the world bust your bubble! Set your goals, step out on that ledge, take a leap of faith, and live out your dreams!

***Living at risk is jumping off the cliff and building your wings on the way down. —Ray Bradbury***

You just cannot allow people to hold you back from what it is you want to achieve. Either they don't have a larger vision for themselves—in which case, it is virtually impossible for them to have a larger vision for you, or they may have a little bit of status over you and don't want to share any of the limelight or run the risk of you surpassing them. One day in 1998, when I was on the bus going to my loss prevention job at TJ Maxx, I ran into a guy I knew from a previous loss prevention job, who we'll call Jake.

While we were on the bus, he told me he had just started working at a newly built Old Navy store in Paramus, New Jersey, and his boss was looking to put together a team of experienced loss prevention agents. Being that I was becoming increasingly unhappy at TJ Maxx, I gave Jake my number and told him to have his boss give me a call. About a week later, I got that call, and about two weeks after that I was working at Old Navy. I took to that job like I did any other; I hit the ground running.

I learned "the Old Navy way" of doing things, and I began doing it to the hilt. Back then, there was a lot of room for growth within the company, and the fact that I was ambitious was a secret to no one. About six months in, I began to notice changes in Jake's behavior. Before I came along, he was the only black guy on the team. However, when I joined the team—because we were both aggressive and had pretty much the same height and build—we became known as the "twin towers."

Even though I respected his position as the assistant loss prevention manager (despite the fact it was never a title officially bestowed upon him), when people began acknowledging us as equals, his attitude toward me really began to change. I also began to notice the sales managers were beginning to treat me differently.

What I later found out from one of the other guys on our team was that Jake was spreading all kinds of nonsense about me to the sales management staff, which laid the groundwork for a few unnecessary conflicts between us. My teammate warned me that Jake was in fact looking to get me fired. Already suspecting this, I assured my buddy there was nothing to worry about. I was, and still am, a stickler for policy; however, the environment Jake was creating was one where I was being made to look totally inflexible.

So, what I did was become totally flexible. Whatever task he assigned; I took without reservation. When I knew he was giving me an assignment that was either counterproductive or just plain didn't make any sense, I still took it in stride with the mind-set that if anyone would have come to me, all I would say was "Jake told me to do it." Personally, I am a staunch advocate of accepting responsibility for one's own actions, but I knew that this man was constantly trying to set me up to fall flat on my face. His biggest concern regarding me was always letting me know who was in charge.

I knew my place, and when asked about certain things, I had no problem telling his superiors that I was just being a "team player" following my team leader! At the same time, I was dealing with Jake's nonsense, I was seeking out new opportunities within the company by interviewing for a lead agent position for a store that was still in the process of being built. When asked in my interview why I wanted to leave such a great store for a smaller location, I simply said, "This is Jake's store. If I'm going to grow in this company, I need to have a store where I can plant my own flag and lead my own team." In the end, I wound up getting that position. Jake, on the other hand, got fired a couple of months later for violating company policies while apprehending a person for shoplifting.

Three months after that, I entered the police academy, and Jake was trying to get a business started training dogs. So, you see, you cannot allow these bubble busters to stand in your way. In the end, however, it is all up to you. You can either allow their negative feedback to deter you from reaching your objectives, or you can convert it into the extra fuel you can use to work that much harder to reach those objectives. There are farms all across America with cows and bulls and horses doing their "doo" all day, every day, and what do those farmers do with all of that "doo?" They take it and put it right back into the soil as fertilizer to keep their crops up.

As a matter of fact, in the early seventies, at the ripe old age of twelve, a young man by the name of Richard Cessna, Jr.—along with his three sisters—created a company called KidCo by cleaning up after horses and selling the manure as fertilizer to landscapers. After a great deal of success, KidCo was taken to court by their adult business rivals and the state tax board. Now, here we have a group of young people doing something constructive and profitable, but when you start dipping into a bubble buster's pockets, they come back at you full force. Apparently the competition pushed that the kids were not paying taxes on the fertilizer they were selling. Their defense? The manure used for fertilizer came from horses fed by Cessna's father, who paid taxes on the feed when he bought it, so how could they tax the feed going in and coming out? But the funny thing is the Cessna children refused an attorney, defended themselves in court, and won!

Bottom line: take what the bubble busters in your life throw your way as the crap it more than likely is and convert it into the fertilizer you need to nurture the planted seeds of your dreams and the fuel you need to press on and fight that much harder.

## Lesson Five: Goals Are What Make the Difference

*Give me a stock clerk with a goal and I will show you*
*a man who will make history. Give me a man*
*without a goal and I will give you a stock clerk.*
*—J.C. Penney*

Now, by the time Taria and I moved into our first
apartment, I was no longer locking up shoplifters at
Old Navy. I had achieved one of my life's goals: I had
become a police officer. As a matter of fact, at that time
in my life, I had four major goals I wanted to achieve
by my thirtieth birthday:

1. *I wanted to be in my chosen career.*
2. *I wanted to find and have the woman I was going*
   *to marry.*
3. *I wanted to drive a nicer car.*
4. *I wanted to move out from under my father's roof*
   *and into a place of my own.*

On August 18, 2000, two months before my thirtieth
birthday, I achieved two of those goals. I graduated
from the police academy, and I proposed to Taria at
my police academy graduation—in front of her family,
my family, and over one hundred and fifty people.
About a little over a month after my birthday, I bought
a nice black '97 Toyota Celica, and about a year and a
half after that, Taria and I moved into our first
apartment.

So, I may not have achieved all of my goals by the time
I had set forth to do so, but I did achieve them
nonetheless. Life gave me what I asked of it, but as I
said earlier, wanting something is not enough. The fact
of the matter is life does not care about what you
want. If that were the case, we would all have a magic
lamp with a genie trapped inside just waiting to give
us those three magical wishes. I did not achieve all of
my goals on or by the exact date I set them for, but

because I had put in the necessary work for them to happen, regardless of the date, they all came to pass relatively close or not too far away from the goal date.

So, I guess you must be asking by now, "So how does life give you what you ask of it if wanting something is not enough?" The answer to that question is this—you must prove your desire and wanting through faith and diligence. This is what I did to achieve my goals and what you must do to achieve yours. As a matter of fact, you will find more often than not that when you actually say, "I want to have _____," or "I want to be _____," all kinds of obstacles begin to drop in front of you. Murphy's Law ("What can go wrong will go wrong, and at the worst possible time") will not only come knocking at your door; it will pitch a tent and camp out in your backyard!

*Nothing on earth can stop the man with the right mental attitude from achieving his goal; nothing on earth can help the man with the wrong mental attitude. —Thomas Jefferson*

So, what do you want out of life? What's the bridge between wanting something and actually getting it? Well, if it's something you just want in terms of "that Bentley sure would look good in my driveway" and the wanting stops there, then what you have is a wish; however, if it is something you want in terms of "I'm going to have that Bentley in my driveway," then at the minimum what you have done is set a goal.

Now, setting goals can be a dangerous thing because the universe is always watching and always listening, and when you say, "This is what I am going to have; this is where I am going to go," or "This is what I am going to be doing," the universe sends Mr. Murphy's Law a "911 page," and he starts packing his bags to pay you a visit. And when he arrives at your doorstep,

Murphy will have a field day making you earn your way while you're trying to find a way.

A great way to fight off Murphy's Law is to build a team or a support system. In today's computer age, with e-mail, two-way texting, teleconferences, video conferences, and so forth, there is really no excuse to not be able to find people who could help and support you toward achieving your goals—even if the only support to be received is moral support. As far as I'm concerned, where two or more are gathered with the shared goal of improving their lives, you've got a team!

In 1997, I was unemployed and looking for work. Although my ultimate long-term goal was to someday become a police officer, my immediate goal was to get a job so I could stop bumming twenty bucks here and there from my father. I had already taken some police exams and was waiting for callbacks, but I needed to pay bills. I was looking for security work, and I got the idea in my head to look into the area of bail enforcement and fugitive recovery—more commonly known as the work of "bounty hunters." I began doing research on how to become a bounty hunter.

I went to the membership directory on America Online, where I found and reached out to people who either were bounty hunters or bail bondsmen. I hooked up with one guy who was from Long Island, New York, who was in the same boat I was in—looking for a way into the business. He also had a security/loss prevention background and wanted to be a police officer. We would look up different Web sites and exchange information with one another on almost a daily basis. One day he sent me the address of one of the regional offices for TJ Maxx, which was in Cherry Hill, New Jersey. I mailed in my résumé with a cover letter and hounded their switchboard for a week until

I was offered a job interview. I was hired on the same day I had my interview.

From TJ Maxx, I went to Old Navy and from there on to achieving my goal of becoming a police officer. Unfortunately, I cannot remember that guy's name. Maybe in the eyes of the universe I was not meant to. Perhaps that guy was just one of God's angels put in my life to serve a specific purpose and then be just a faint memory. I came across someone who shared my goals and my vision, and he helped put me on a path that has brought me to a wonderful place. When you have a goal, you not only have a destination to reach, but you have a journey from which to learn all kinds of things on your way to reaching that destination. If you fail to set goals, then you fail to move onward to greatness.

There is no such thing as a stagnant journey. You're either going somewhere or you're not. Zig Ziglar says that when we are on the journey toward achieving our goals, one of the best things we can do is "see the reaching." No matter how far the road ahead may seem, we should always go as far ahead as we can see, and when we get there, we will always be able to see farther. Just keep on going. If you have a goal, then you already know what's waiting for you at the end of the road.

The scary part is the journey getting there because there will be times when you won't be able to see the road ahead. There will be times when you will have to face the unknown. Even though it is human nature to fear the unknown, it goes against the human spirit, and the will of the successful succumbs to that fear. Just remember that facing the unknown is not a reasonable act. It is a necessary one in order to succeed.

*A man or a woman without a goal is like a ship without a rudder. Each will drift and not drive. Each will end up on the beaches of despair, defeat, and despondency. —Zig Ziglar*

*The road to success is always under construction. It is a progressive course, not an end to be reached. —Anthony Robbins*

*You're either on the way, or you're in the way! —Les Brown*

It would be nice if we could just turn on a magic faucet or open a magic door and be able to have everything we ever wanted, but life just does not work that way. We have to make our own magic in our lifetimes. The very first step in creating your own magic is for you to sit down and create some goals. This is not a difficult process either. You don't have to want to be the greatest singer or athlete, especially if you're not already working toward it. Your first set of goals should be reasonable things.

Again, for me when I was in my mid-twenties, I had set the following goals for myself to achieve by my thirtieth birthday:

1. *I wanted to be in my chosen career.*
2. *I wanted to find and have the woman I was going to marry.*
3. *I wanted to drive a nicer car.*
4. *I wanted to move out from under my father's roof and into a place of my own.*

Achieving those goals was by no means easy, but I cannot begin to think where I would be had I not created them and worked to follow through on them. In other words, goals are what make the difference because goals give meaning to your life. Create reasonable goals but be completely unreasonable in seeing them through. Ask yourself, "Why am I here?"

Recognize that life will give you what you ask of it—provided you have the courage to ask!

Recognize that if your goal is something you really want and it is something really worth having or achieving, it's not going to come easy. You're going to have to put in some work and endure some patches of rough road along the way. Don't worry, though; the bubble busters in your life will make themselves known and provide that for you. In the end it's going to be those goals that will see you through and to the end.

Your goals give you purpose. So how do you set your goals? Well, take a long, deep, and honest look at your life. Think about the changes you want to make and then write them down. Let me repeat that—write them down! There is very little commitment in a goal wrapped in thought. When you write something down, you make it tangible.

There's a rule in writing police reports that can be applied to this point: "If it's not written down in black and white, it never happened." If you're new to writing down your goals, you don't have to start out with "I want to tell Donald Trump he's fired!" Start with something small and immediately achievable. A small victory is still a victory as far as I'm concerned. And when you develop a habit out of enjoying small victories, your confidence builds up and you become bolder. When that happens, you feel more confident in setting bigger and bigger goals.

So, what are some small things you want to do? Clean your room. Straighten out your desk. What are some big things? Pay off your debts. Find the man or woman of your dreams. Start your own business. Start creating some goals, and even more important, start working toward achieving them. If you already have nothing, what do you have to lose? The next thing you want to do is go to the office supply store and get yourself some index cards, a box or two of pushpins, and a corkboard like the kind you used for a bulletin board in school. You're going to use the index cards to write down your goals, and then you're going to put those cards everywhere you are—by your bedside, on your mirror in the bathroom, at your desk at work.

Put those cards wherever you are or are going to be so that you can pull them out and reaffirm those goals to yourself whenever and wherever the mood strikes you— which should be all the time and everywhere! As for the corkboard and pushpins, this is where the fun part of goal setting comes in. You see it's one thing to write down, "I want to have a new Corvette," yet it's another to see yourself in that Corvette. So, take that corkboard and put it up in your home office, den, bedroom, or any place in your home that is just your space.

The next thing you're going to do is get pictures of whatever it is you are setting as your goal and put them up on that board. Every day look at that board and see yourself in that mansion. See yourself in that car. See yourself with those washboard abs. See yourself in those designer suits and dresses. See yourself being who, what, and where you want to be!

*The difference between the optimist and the pessimist is that the pessimist says, "I'll believe it when I see it," while the optimist says, "I'll see it when I believe it." —Robert Schuller*

Writing this book was by no means an easy process, especially since a great many of these lessons stem from hardships I have endured during my short and humbling journey—which is by no means anywhere near over. The fact you have this book in your hands is the manifestation of my optimism and goal setting. If you bought this book in a bookstore, then you are a witness to the power of goal setting.

When I first wrote and released this book, I was just looking to be able to sell this book out of the trunk of my car or from wherever I may have been speaking. This leads me to another point. Be reasonable when setting your goals, be unreasonable while on your way to reaching them, but all throughout, be patient. This is what will be the most difficult thing for you to do in achieving your goals. Remember the previous lesson—nothing worth having comes easy, and patience is a virtue no one can afford to do without while pursuing one's goals. I know of this personally because I am guilty of being impatient while pursuing my goals.

Even more difficult than being patient while waiting for your goals to manifest themselves into reality is to know when you just might have to let go. However, if you are true to yourself throughout the entire process, if you feel and believe that this particular goal is what is meant to be yours, keep in mind that—as I've said and shall say again—the universe is watching, and the universe, no, God is watching and also knows what is pure in your heart. I submit to you that if the goal you set is pure and you do what is required, but by the grace of God, you shall have it!

## Lesson Six: You Have To Prove Yourself

*As you continue your journey to the top, you must remember that each rung of the ladder was placed there for the purpose of holding your foot just long enough to step higher. It wasn't put there for you to rest on. —Zig Ziglar*

*As you continue your journey to the top, you must remember that each rung of the ladder was placed there for the purpose of holding your foot just long enough to step higher. It wasn't put there for you to rest on. —Zig Ziglar*

*No matter how many times you are "down," you are not whipped if you get up one more time than you are knocked down. —Zig Ziglar*

I love my father dearly, but my father can be a very negative person at times. The gentlest way I can describe him is as either a "pessimistic realist" or a "realistic pessimist." He will be the first one to point out every single negative aspect of a given situation and how something, anything, could go wrong. One of his favorite sayings is, "The best laid plans of mice and men often go awry." The funny thing is, I learned so much from that negativity.

For one thing, I learned that he does what works for him. I also learned that he never wished failure upon a person; he would just be the one to say, "I knew it," if things did not turn out right. My father is happy in his comfort zone and rarely goes outside of it unless it works for him to do so. When I was in high school, I played football my freshman year ... wait a minute ... let me rephrase that—I was on the football team my freshman year. However, even though I was a first-string bench warmer for 99% of the season, my father was at every game. For eight weeks, my father kept telling me, "Just work harder and show the coach you want to play." That was really good advice, but the fact of the matter was I really did not want to play.

The reality of the matter was that I had joined the football team for him, and the reason that I did not play was because I did not deserve to play. I did not put forth my best effort, and there were guys there who really did want to play and were better on the field than me, and they were the ones who got in the game. I remember skipping practice for an entire week, but on game day I still showed up and suited up. One of the assistant coaches even approached me and said, "Reed, you've got some nerve coming here expecting to play after cutting practice all week!" I told him, "I don't expect to play, but my father is going to be out there." The coach just shrugged his shoulders and walked away.

On a bright note, I did eventually get to play. It was the last game of the season, two minutes left in the game, and we had something like a twenty-one-point lead. It was not that big a deal to me, but for those two minutes, my father was ecstatic. All throughout the season and up until the end, the truth of the matter was I had never proven myself to the coach, so I became a liability to the team's chances of winning and thus was not allowed to play until my participation was virtually worthless either way.

*In the eyes of the universe, if you do not prove yourself to yourself, then you become a liability to your chances of victory and success. —HSRjr*

I did not return to the gridiron in my sophomore year. My art teacher, Mr. George LaTorre, who was also the coach of the fencing team, asked me to try out, and I wound up enjoying it. My father, on the other hand, was not as enthused. During my sophomore year, I was on the junior varsity team, but he did not come out to a single match. At first I resented him for it, but I also realized that he may have been upset that I was beginning to exercise some small measure of independence. I played football; rather, I joined the football team for him, but I joined the fencing team for me. Also, unlike on the football team, Mr. LaTorre saw to it that everybody got to participate at some level. We had enough talent to have a strong team to compete, but the coach would also ask the opposing teams if they had freshman or J.V. fencers who they wanted to get some competitive experience even if the matches were not official. So, if we had an awesome lead, guys with less experience got to compete, and if we were at the point where a loss was imminent and we had a better chance of catching a fart in the wind than beating the other team, guys with less experience still got to compete.

So, I began to learn the sport, and being tall, long, lanky, and quick, I learned I had the makings of a good fencer. During my junior year, I began to come into my own. I made the varsity epee' squad, I was competing regularly at both team matches and tournaments, and I was getting quite a few individual wins under my belt. My father, however, was still not very supportive, but he was beginning to see the effort I was putting out. By the end of the season, my team had gone undefeated against every school we faced, we won every major tournament including the state championships, and I even got my name in the paper a couple of times. I even qualified as an alternate for the Junior Olympics in Orlando, Florida; however, it was one of my aunts and my grandparents who gave me the money to go.

During my senior year, I had gotten a lot better; we repeated the undefeated winning streak (with the exception of one tournament that, even though we placed second, we turned into a positive by accepting it as a well-deserved humbling experience), and being that we were winning and I was getting my name in the paper for having won a couple of matches that led to overall team victories, my father started coming out and showing up at some of the home matches. Whereas during my junior year I only made it to the Junior Olympics as an alternate, in my senior year I qualified to actually compete. My team had been doing so well that the school paid our way, but at least for this trip, my father gave me some spending money! He even came out to the state championship tournament—our final tournament and my last as a high school fencer, and he cheered for me while asking my teammates questions about how the matches were judged and scored (we won that tournament too)!

About a week later, when he read in the paper that I made the 1987–88 All-State Team, he was on cloud nine! Over my last two years of high school fencing, I had amassed quite a collection of medals that my father had begun to proudly display in the living room right alongside some of his most prized college fraternity paraphernalia. I remember being bored one Saturday and saying to myself, "I won these medals … they should be on my wall!" and I took them down from the mantel in the living room and put them up on a wall in my room above my bed. When my father came home and saw those medals taken down, he flat out demanded that I put them right back where they were—as if he had won them! To this day, even though I have my own home, those medals remain on his mantel.

However, it was then that I realized I had proven myself to him and he really was proud of what I had accomplished (on a side note, the football team never went undefeated, let alone ever won a state championship tournament)! What I began realizing is that my father held me accountable to whatever it was I said I was going to do, and if I were to come up short, then I would have to hear it from him to almost no end. So, what I began to do from that day on was plan my work and work my plan, and I would only make my actions known to him when I had something worthy of showing. If in the process of trying to do something it did not work out, no big deal … back to the drawing board, and that's how life works. Like I said, life does not care about what you want. Life only cares about what you are willing to do to prove you are worthy of having or being what it is that you want.

When you are in pursuit of your goals, the universe is going to test you over and over again. Sometimes you will feel as though when you make one strong step forward life is either knocking you back two steps or just knocking you down on your butt, but like Les Brown says, "When life knocks you down—and it will—try to land on your back, because if you can look up you can get up!"

*For the first 80% of the time that you are working toward your goal, you will only cover about 20% of the distance. However, if you persist and refuse to give up, you will accomplish the final 80% of your goal in the last 20% of the time you spend working it. —Brian Tracy*

Worthy objectives are not meant to be easily achieved. You have to be unreasonably tenacious in striving for your goals. You might be going out to get a new job or a higher position in your current career. Unless you are your own boss, you are going to have to prove yourself to be an asset to your boss. Ultimately, you don't want your boss to be threatened by your ambition, but at the same time there is nothing wrong with being ambitious. When I was going through my ordeal at Old Navy with my supervisor, Jake, I knew it was because I had already proven myself to be a threat to him and his ambitions.

However, I did not rise to the top of that situation by going head to head with him on his team. I rose to the top of that situation by proving myself to be an asset to the company by conducting myself in the manner that was expected by his bosses. I took the initiative to compile all of the lessons I had learned in my previous loss prevention jobs and create a Loss Prevention Training Manual. I doubt they're still using it, but it impressed the regional sales and loss prevention managers enough to fly me out to one of the new stores built in Maryland to train two newly hired loss prevention agents. One of my favorite memories of working there was finding how heated Jake got when he found out he was not even considered for that assignment. A month later, I was leading my own team in my own store.

*Though no one can go back and make a brand new start, anyone can start from now and make a brand new ending. —Carl Bard*

I probably could have gone on bumping heads with Jake and beaten him. I actually kept a journal of his little misdeeds and shortcuts and probably could have started talking about him behind his back and beaten him by ratting him out. However, something divine entered my mind and forced me to find a more honorable solution. Several months after leaving the company, I ran into one of the sales managers I used to work with who told me that a few of them (the other sales managers) had known Jake was jealous of my ambition and was possibly trying to sabotage my career; however, they were more interested in seeing how I handled the situation than they were in trying to step in and mediate some kind of resolution between us.

I learned they appreciated the fact that the more Jake came at me, I would handle each situation with more silent humility and professionalism than the previous situation. After a while, my star began to rise and his began to fade ... all the way up to me eventually moving on to the career we both wanted, while he wound up losing his job. In this case, the managers were playing the role of the universe. Just as the universe had been watching me all along, they were observing two ambitious men.

Jake's goal was to crush, humiliate, and remove me, while my goal was to rise above his petty behavior, remove him from my radar, and succeed in spite of him. I proved myself worthy to the managers, and they elevated me to a better position. I proved myself to the universe, and it saw me through to achieving my ultimate goal!

*If you have a positive attitude and constantly strive to give your best effort, eventually you will overcome your immediate problems and find you are ready for greater challenges. —Pat Riley*

## Lesson Seven: "The Journey of a Thousand Miles..."

*Initiating an active change in your life is like an airplane taking off ... There will be turbulence before you reach a comfortable altitude.*
*—Les Brown*

"The journey of a thousand miles begins with a single step." This is one of the greatest quotes ever recorded by the Chinese philosopher Confucius. Success does not just land in your lap. It comes to those who go after it. No one just "finds" a hidden treasure; after all, it's "hidden." So, in order for it to be found, one must go looking for it. Even if you are standing on the very spot where the treasure is hidden, you will still have to dig to get to it.

If you are not willing to get dirty and dig for that treasure, it does not matter if the treasure is buried five feet or five hundred feet beneath you. If you are not willing to do what is required to get that treasure, even with the opportunity to get it staring you in the face, it shall never be yours. This is how life works. As much as I am personally opposed to playing the lottery, the same principle applies. If you never scratch that ticket, it's a guarantee that you're never going to win the prize.

*Only those who will risk going too far can possibly find out how far one can go. —S. Eliot*

In life, when you put your very best into a task, your chances of success are greater than if you just try to skate by. Don't we all know someone who we either work with or went to school with who seemed to be the luckiest person around? They seem to catch all the breaks, but you know that they aren't doing much, if anything, more than you are. My wife, Taria, was in such a position once. She had a job where the people in her office really took advantage of her kindness and her eagerness to work. Almost weekly she would complain about someone dumping their work on her.

I advised her to just stay the course and do the job. Knowing that she worked for a company that was Japanese-owned and knowing that every so often the big wigs do come down from up high and do hands-on, fine tooth comb inspections, I told her that eventually there would come a time when people would have to show and prove they were up to snuff, and if the people in her department really were dumping their work on her and not doing their share, it would definitely come to light when those inspectors showed up. A few months later, that's exactly what happened, and within two weeks from that visit, everyone in her department—except her—was replaced. She wound up staying there and practically running her department (unfortunately, she wasn't paid comparably for doing so).

Now, had she just become a complainer instead of digging in when she did, she could have fallen victim to the "spring cleaning" that took place. However, when the struggle first reared its ugly head, she dug in and held her ground—day after day, week after week, and month after month until vindication was hers. The day she went back to work, after I advised her to change her outlook on the job, was when she took the first step, and even though she had quite a few obstacles to overcome, when she reached the end of that particular road, she was the one who came out on top.

It does not matter what it is that you want to do. If you do nothing but say, "Someday, I'm gonna ..." in reality, you're never gonna. I remember telling myself for three years in a row that I was going to drop a few pounds and tone up. And for three years in a row, the weight would fluctuate, but then I never quite got to where I wanted to be. I figured I would change my tactics up and just do little things with the hopes that down the line they would add up. In 2005, I swore off McDonald's, and I was doing great until I was at a convention in Atlantic City that summer and found myself hungry at three o'clock in the morning with nothing in walking distance but McDonald's.

My journey started on January 1 and ended on July 23. Once I got home, when those fries called out my name, I answered. However, when 2006 rolled around, I swore off McDonald's again; hence, my journey began again. I am proud to say that as I write this particular paragraph, I have been entirely "Mickey Dee's" free all year long (and since I've just put that in print, I'm going to use that as a reinforcement to stay the course). Next year I might go back to McDonald's (in moderation) and swear off Burger King. Who knows? The bottom line is you will never reach your destination if you don't make a move at all. In the end, it really does not matter what you want to do in life. If you do not act toward achieving what you want, then you'll just be wanting for the rest of your life.

*Desire is the key to motivation, but it's determination and commitment to an unrelenting pursuit of your goal—a commitment to excellence— that will enable you to attain the success you seek. —Mario Andretti*

What do you want to do with your life? What do you want to achieve? Do you want to lose twenty pounds? Do you want to tone up and add muscle to your body? Do you want to be able to run a four-minute mile? Do you want to become a lawyer or a doctor? These are all worthy goals to achieve; however, you can't just up and say, "I'm a doctor," and make it so. It takes four years of college, four years of medical school, and at least three years working in a hospital. Talk about "a journey of a thousand miles"; that's 4,015 days—

including weekends! You have to take that first step, and that first step is the hardest one to take.

Once you've taken that step, even though the next few may be hard as well, after a while, you've got a stroll going on. A while after that you've got a natural rhythm going; you're strutting along your way looking like John Travolta in Saturday Night Fever! The best way to do something a million and one times is to just do it once. Just do it once. If you want to be able to do fifty push-ups but cannot even do ten, start by doing five in the morning when you get out of bed and then five at night before you go to bed. Then look at what you've done—you've done ten push-ups for the day! You have got nothing to prove to anyone but yourself, so all that matters is that you did those ten.

Now, after about a week or two, you might even be able to do ten push-ups in the morning and another ten at night. Wow—you're just a little shy of being halfway to your goal! How about during that third or fourth week you throw in another set of ten when you get home from work in between the time you take off your work clothes and put on your bum-around-the-house clothes? I'll just about bet that after about a month and a half, if you were not in too bad shape to begin with, you just might be able to bang out one solid set of fifty push-ups. If not, so what? What is important is that you started on your journey to getting there.

When I started the police academy in February of 2000, I was not in the best shape. The standard time to run a mile and a half for a person my age back then was twelve minutes. The first time I ran that course, it took me twenty-two minutes. What's worse is that about four weeks later I had to withdraw from the academy because I had developed shin splints in both legs, and it was getting to the point where I could barely walk, let alone run. However, this was nothing more than an obstacle to be overcome. I had to take about a month and a half off (without pay) while my legs healed. When I returned to the academy, I had to start all over again from day one! Talk about a journey of a thousand miles! But in the end, by August, I was able to shave those twenty-two minutes down to eleven (by now, I'm probably back at twenty-two minutes)! Seriously, the point is if I had given up I never would have been able to make such an accomplishment.

As I write this page and look back, that was some seven years ago. I weighed about 204 pounds. Now, I'm 2#@ pounds (smile) and nowhere near capable of making that run in that time at this point in time. However, if I ever decided to drop some pounds and/or even make that run time again—and I just might, the most important thing I must do is start doing it! Two of the most significant experiences in my life were the six weeks I spent in boot camp for the U.S. Air Force and the several weeks I spent pledging into the most distinguished fraternal organization around, otherwise known as Groove Phi Groove Social Fellowship Incorporated. These experiences were the most significant because they best taught me the power of both physical and mental endurance.

Of the many things I learned from both experiences, what they equally shared was the fact that when one day ended, that was one less day I had to worry about, and one day closer I was to achieving my goal. No matter what I endured on Monday, when Tuesday came, there was nothing that Monday could do to hurt me, and I knew that Tuesday couldn't hang around forever!

### *The Four-Cycle Pledge Process*

When I thought back on all that I endured on my journey to become a member of the fellowship, I asked myself how could I best describe the journey with the fewest words possible, and this is what I came up with:

1. I started something with the mind-set to finish it.

2. I endured the process with the mind-set to finish it.

3. I finished it.

4. I started something new with the mind-set to finish it.

Originally I was just looking for a way to describe my pledge process, but in the end I came to the realization that life is a four-cycle pledge process. There is not one single thing in my life that I have fully engaged in that does not follow this particular hypothesis—to include life itself. Think about it. Our parents make/start us, we're born, we live, we die, we move on. We go to school (oh boy!), we endure school, we graduate or leave, we go out into the work force. Look at it on an even larger scale: we're goofy little babies, then we go to school, then we go to work, then we retire! So, whether you recognize it or not, you have been on a journey ever since the day your parents conceived you.

At the very beginning of that journey, from your father's end, you had four hundred to five hundred million traveling companions, but in the end you were the only one to make it! Out of five hundred million possible outcomes, you were the winning one—how could you not be destined for greatness? Just like the earth itself, this journey we call life is chock-full of bumpy roads and rough terrain. There will be obstacles in your path that you may be capable of overcoming, and others you may have to figure out a way to go around. Before this journey ends, you are going to make some wrong turns.

You might wind up on a couple of dead-end streets, but you can always turn around, go back the way you came, and find another path. One thing is certain—your journeys will come to an end. How they end will be determined by what you learned along the way and how you incorporated it into your journey. You may not get it 100 percent right every time, but you've got to keep on walking! Michael Jordan and Larry Bird missed more shots than they made, and Reggie Jackson and Babe Ruth struck out more times than they hit home runs, and they were the greatest in their given sports. So, I ask you again, what do you want to do with your life? Take some time and figure it out, and when you do, take the first step and get started on your thousand miles!

## *Lesson Eight: Procrastination Gives You Psychic Ability!*

### *Procrastination is like masturbation; in the end, you're just screwing yourself! —Unknown*

Procrastination gives you psychic ability! How can I say this? Well, look at it like this—you say you want to do something, or even worse you know you have to do something. By invoking the power of procrastination, you are granted the power to predict that you will not accomplish what you want or have to do. I have learned that the two major forces that guide our lives are pain and pleasure, and the reality is we work harder to avoid pain than we do to seek pleasure.

Don't believe me? How many people do you know who try to think out different ways to avoid paying for a speeding ticket as opposed to just driving like they have some sense in the first place? Let's say you've got a report to do for work or school, you've got a month to do it even though it would only take you two weeks, but at the same time you know you really don't want to do it at all (this is the pain). More often than not, the average person will put off getting the report done for the first week or two (as a means to avoid the pain) and then cram to get it done during the last week or two and probably come up with a substandard report. The reality is it would have been less painful and more pleasurable to do the report during the first two weeks and coast for the remaining two weeks.

If you say, "I want to lose twenty pounds by the end of the year" but do nothing toward achieving that goal, you can predict with absolute certainty you will not lose those twenty pounds—and you might gain five more. Trust me—I know this! If you see an attractive person that you want to get to know (who does not know you even exist) but don't step to them to even say "hello," you can predict with absolute certainty that the next arm you see them on will not be yours.

To touch back on a previous lesson, remember what the great Chinese philosopher Confucius said: "The journey of a thousand miles begins with the first step." You cannot graduate college if you don't enroll. You cannot learn the knowledge contained within a book if you never crack the cover.

This I know from personal knowledge. I bought the book Unlimited Power by Tony Robbins in 1988, but I did not actually buckle down and read it from cover to cover until 1998. That book opened my mind to a whole new way of seeing life and dealing with people. The reality is I cheated myself out of ten years' worth of different unknown possibilities that could have made my bumpy roads easier.

*Procrastination usually results in sorrowful regret. Today's duties put off until tomorrow give us a double burden to bear; the best way to do them is in proper time. —Ida Scott Taylor*

By procrastinating to open that book and read it through, I inadvertently predicted I would not be able to benefit from the knowledge contained within it. Do you hate going to the gym or lifting at home if you own your own weights? I know I do, but I feel great after a good workout, don't you? I hate running, but when I can get myself to get up off my bottom and do at least a mile or two on the track or treadmill, I feel like I've accomplished something. It's a very rare thing for procrastination to actually serve a positive purpose.

For one to be a self-admitted procrastinator is for that same person to look you square in the eye and say, "Hey, I just thought you should know from the start that I am unreliable." I used to even joke with one of my closest friends and tell him that the only thing he was reliable at was being unreliable. In every good lie and every good joke, there is always a shred of truth, and we both always got a good laugh out of that, but I have to honestly say if I ever called him and really needed him in a clinch, he was there! It was not that he was unreliable. He was just a procrastinator. A person procrastinates because whatever it is that needs to be done is just not important enough for him or her to do right then and there.

How many times did your parent or wife or husband ask you to do some menial chore around the house like wash the dishes, put away the laundry, or clean up a particular room, and even though you acknowledged that you would do it, you didn't stop whatever it was you were doing at that moment to complete the requested task? Be honest, how many times did you say, "I'll get to it in a few minutes," and a few minutes turned into a few hours then perhaps a few days? Now let me ask you this: how many times were you asked to complete a task and offered some kind of compensation for completing the task?

Whether the compensation was money, a night out dancing or having dinner, or some "special attention" from your mate, all you had to do was complete the task in the time requested by the other person. How long would it take you to complete that task? Not long, I bet. For kids, there are four places that jump into my head that will get a kid up and burning: the toy store, McDonald's, Burger King, and of course Disneyland. If you want a kid to get something done—anything from keeping his or her room clean to chipping in with the household chores to doing well in school—if you promise one of those things as a reward for a desired activity or behavior, I just about guarantee you that the kid is going to perform.

You see, the reward or compensation is the "pleasure" I was talking about. When we are going along doing our own thing, we are somewhat in a state of pleasure, not a state of euphoria, but we're just content in our own space doing our own thing, and when someone else comes along and busts up that groove with some request or assignment that was not in our original game plan, well, that's "pain"—not excruciating pain, but an annoyance. The new task or assignment may very well be important to the other person, but it's not important to you—at least not at that particular moment—so you put it off. You might not feel like taking the garbage out today, but if today is Monday, chances are by Wednesday it's going to be pretty important to you!

If your parent or spouse asked you to take out the garbage on Monday and you decided to wait until Wednesday, you can predict you might be host to a party of a few multi-legged friends looking for a free meal. I cannot tell you how many times I have had an encounter where I was supposed to do something, and I put it off. You don't necessarily have to jump on every single task as soon as it comes up, but one must learn the art of prioritization.

Prioritizing can conquer procrastination, but you can't just put things in a certain order to be accomplished without committing to completing them all. If you have five or six things to do and put them all off, you are procrastinating in the worst way. If you take those five or six tasks, prioritize them in order of importance, and then put them off anyway, you have not really created any benefit for yourself. In fact, you have wasted even more time! However, if you chunk that entire list as one task consisting of several parts and you get to work on the first task on that list then the next, before you know it, you'll be complete with all of those tasks!

***Procrastination is the graveyard of time.***
***—Unknown***

We are all guilty of procrastination, but what we must realize is that although not every task is a code-red high priority, that is no excuse for sheer laziness, and more often than not the cause of procrastination has more to do with laziness than it does priority. Procrastination is a bad habit, and like any bad habit, with commitment and conscious, consistent effort, it is one that can be broken. Zig Ziglar says, "When you choose a habit, you also choose the end result of that habit." So, when you choose to be a procrastinator, you also choose to be labeled as irresponsible and/or unreliable.

***Habit is a cable; we weave a thread of it each day until it becomes too strong to break. Then the strength of that cable either takes us to the top—or ties us to the bottom depending on whether it is a good one or a bad one. —Zig Ziglar***

It's not enough to know your purpose and set a goal if you are not willing to take the necessary action to manifest that goal into a reality. It does not matter if your friends and family support you or not if you keep putting off taking that first step. As a matter of fact, with every passing day you procrastinate, you not only predict your eventual failure, you also prove that those bubble busters in your life were right all along.

When you procrastinate, you fail to prove yourself worthy of the goals you wish to accomplish because the testing and obstacles that you have to overcome won't even come your way until you take action. Like the hockey great Wayne Gretsky said, "You will miss 100% of the shots you never take." The bottom line is, when you know there is something you have to do—or even better something you want to do—get off your bottom and do what has to be done. You'll be glad that you did when you're sitting back relaxing while everyone else who chose to procrastinate fulfills their own pain-filled prophecies.

# Lesson Nine: Mistakes Are a Gift from God

*While one person hesitates because he feels inferior, the other is busy making mistakes and becoming superior. —Henry C. Link*

A "mistake" is defined as an error in action, calculation, opinion, or judgment caused by poor reasoning, carelessness, insufficient knowledge, etc. Being that none of us are perfect, the fact of the matter is that in life mistakes do happen. They happen every day by just about everyone. If you have ever met a person who claims to have never made a mistake, my advice to you is to turn away and run for your life because that person is long overdue!

*A life spent making mistakes is not only more honorable, but more useful than a life spent doing nothing. —George Bernard Shaw*

Now, I'm going to tell you something about mistakes that you've probably never heard—mistakes are a gift from God! I would even dare to say that they are baby miracles, but here is the kicker: you have to learn from the mistake and not repeat the mistake under similar circumstances for the miracle to actually take effect, and since history has a way of repeating itself, I can guarantee you that you will always be faced with similar circumstances. So bear in mind the old saying, those who don't learn from history's mistakes are doomed to repeat them.

## So How Do We Learn From Our Mistakes?

The answer is so simple that it is virtually invisible. In order to learn from your mistakes, you have to first hold yourself accountable and acknowledge that you made a mistake in the first place. We all have either experienced or been told a story about that three-year-old whose mother warned him or her about touching a hot stove or pot. The three-year-old, being a three-year-old, goes right on ahead and touches that hot stove or pot anyway and … ouch! That sting or even blister was all the acknowledgment in the world that child needed to know he or she made a mistake and more than likely never repeated it. So, once you've acknowledged that you have made a mistake, the next step is to not do it again! You see, it's all about consequences.

The reason why there is such apathy and such a lack of respect for authority in today's society—and especially amongst our youth—is there is little to no regard for the concept of consequences. People see me as a police officer, and the most common thing they will say is, "You can do whatever you want because you have that badge and that gun." In response, I often tell them that it is exactly because of those particular items that I cannot do whatever I want.

You see, it's a part of my profession to know the law and thus the consequences for violating it, and because I know the consequence of my actions, I know not only what to do and what not to do, but how to go about conducting myself properly and thus improve my chances to avoid making mistakes. Yet, I digress, as this is not so much about knowing the difference between right and wrong as it is about increasing your chances to do right by minimizing your chances of doing wrong.

*While we are free to choose our actions, we are not free to choose the consequences of our actions.*
*—Steven R. Covey*

I remember a significant mistake I made back when I was around maybe eight or nine years old. Every day after school, I was supposed to get on a bus and go to an afterschool day care program with the YMCA. I think my mother was paying something like $30 a week for me to go there. There were plenty of activities to be engaged in after completing our homework, and then somewhere around 6:00 p.m., some parents would come pick their kids up or a bus would take us home. I was one of the kids who would take the bus home. Well, I decided to play hooky from the Y and go to my friend Juan's house and play.

I had a ball, and since Juan only lived about a ten-minute walk away, I was still able to safely get home around the same time I would have had I been brought home by the bus. Now, I did this just about every day for about a month without getting caught. So, what does a person typically do when they're doing something wrong and not getting caught? Right—they keep on doing it! Well, I was no different, and everything had come to a head when my mother got a letter in the mail from the Y. Actually, I believe it might have been both a letter and her check that she had sent in earlier that week or the week before. The letter explained they were returning her check because I had not been there for just about the entire month. It was just my luck that she got that letter on a Friday, but she didn't say anything about it until Saturday.

Here's how it went down: every Saturday morning I would get up, wash up, make myself some cereal, and watch cartoons. After the cartoons, I would either play with my toys, read comic books, go outside and play, or all of the above. On this particular Saturday, Juan and some more of my friends from school had come to my house to get me. I could hear them out in the street when they were on their way, so I started getting ready by putting my sneakers on while asking my mother if I could go out and play. She acted like she didn't hear me, but when my buddies rang the doorbell, she told me to go in the kitchen and sit down. She opened the door, and when my buddies said, "Hi, Mrs. Reed. Can Harold come outside?" she said, "I don't know yet. Tell me something. When you guys get out of school, does Harold get on the bus and go to the Y?"

My best buddy, Juan, who could never lie to save his life, with a big smile on his face, said, "Well, he used to, but now he just comes over to my house to play after school!" My mother then said, "Well, Harold won't be able to come outside. He will see you in school on Monday. Bye, boys." When I heard Juan answer my mother, I knew my fate was sealed. I felt like my heart and my lungs dropped to the bottom of my stomach. When my mother came into the kitchen, she said, "So you want to waste my money playing hooky? Go into the bedroom and take your clothes off." Now, I knew a whooping was coming, but normally in these instances she would say, "Drop your pants." Let's just say I got a whooping of galactic proportions, and I never missed that bus to the Y ever again!

### Why Do We Make Mistakes, and What Do We Do To Prevent Making Them In The Future?

It was Les Brown who said, "The best way to get back on your feet is to miss two car payments!" Missing the payment is the mistake, and having your car repossessed is the consequence. If you are fortunate enough to get your car back or you are able to get another car and succeed at making the remainder of your payments on time, congratulations! Lesson learned! Where do mistakes come from? In a word … ignorance.

Sometimes we make a mistake because we just did not know any better. Sometimes we may have forgotten to do something. More often than we are willing to admit, however, we make mistakes because we just didn't think! In the fall and winter of 2006 through early 2007, all throughout Middlesex County, towns had experienced a rash of break-ins to cars where most of the time the only thing that was taken was the Global

Positioning System (GPS) that the driver left either on the dashboard or attached to the inside of the windshield by a suction cup.

When I had to do a theft report for victims of this crime, I would politely ask the person, "Would you leave $500 in cash on your dashboard?" Of course, the person would say no. Then I would ask, "Would you leave your wife's wedding ring on the dashboard or a $2,000 set of golf clubs in plain view in the back seat?" The answer again, "No." Finally I would ask, "So why would you leave your GPS in plain sight on the dashboard or attached to the windshield?" The response nine times out of ten, "I didn't think anyone would steal it." At that point (depending on the person's demeanor at the time), I might say to him or her, "I'm sorry, what were the first three words of the last thing you just said?"

The person would then pause, think back, and then slowly say, "I ... didn't ... think." How many times has someone explained themselves or you yourself explained actions by saying, "I didn't think it had to be done that way"? The most important portion of that sentence is the words "I didn't think." Once you have said those three magic words, you have confessed your ignorance. Now, depending on the nature of the mistake and/or the gravity of the consequences, the mistake might not be that big of a deal; however, if one does not attempt to learn from that little mistake, the next time around, the end result could be disastrous.

You might make the mistake of not looking both ways before crossing the street or pulling out into traffic and just narrowly miss being hit by a car or causing a collision. Making that same mistake the next time around could possibly end up with you meeting the business end of a Buick or engaging in an immediate and unexpected introduction to Mr. Airbag (I know this from personal experience, and although I hated meeting him, I was glad he was there).

*Do not fall victim to the concept of "common sense," for if common sense was in fact "common," everyone would have it. —HSRjr*

Like I said in the beginning, mistakes do happen, and at some point in time, we are all going to share in the experience. The best way to avoid making a mistake is to pay attention to what it is you're doing or have to do. In the Air Force, I learned the significance of paying attention to detail, and, particularly in boot camp, I learned that anything worth doing is worth doing right the first time. Any time one of my boot-mates would shirk the tiniest aspect of a task, that particular detail would always be the thing that caught the drill instructor's attention.

This leads me to another point. Mistakes also come from a lack of paying attention to detail, otherwise known as a lapse in judgment. When you intentionally neglect a particular detail or you are in such a rush that you don't put in the quality of time necessary to do the job right, things will go awry more often than they will run smoothly.

### How Do We Turn a Negative Into a Positive?

As I said, mistakes are gifts from God, like baby miracles, but you have to learn from them in order for the miracle to manifest itself. The great thing about it is that the mistakes you learn from don't even have to be your mistakes to learn from. How many times have you had a spirited debate with your parents about wanting to go to a party or hang out with your friends or wear a certain pair of jeans because "everyone else is doing it," only to have your parents end (and win) the debate by asking, "If your friends jump off a cliff, are you going to jump too?" If you want to learn from others' mistakes, it's not a hard thing to do. You can go to an Alcoholics Anonymous (www.alcoholics-anonymous.org) meeting and hear all kinds of horror stories about how the abuse of alcohol has ruined many lives on many different levels.

The same applies for drug abuse (Narcotics Anonymous—www. na.org) and gambling (Gamblers Anonymous—www. gamblersanonymous.org). If you think it is only in the movies where people talk about how the monkey was so heavy on their back that they would sell their most cherished belongings, their bodies, and even their children to get that next "fix," find out where a meeting is, attend, and get a nice dish of reality served cold. You can leave the bar knowing you have no business being behind the wheel and get home by the grace of God, but so many times God might find himself running a little low on angels and decide it's time to call a couple of souls home, but at the same time, he might decide that you need to be taught a lesson.

So, take you getting behind the wheel drunk and add that to an elderly couple driving home from the weekly date that they never missed, going on in fifty years of marriage, and smash! God has his angels, and you have hit rock bottom. Driving while intoxicated, two counts of vehicular manslaughter, a multimillion dollar lawsuit, and responsibility for the overall disgrace of your entire family. It should not take a "mistake" of that magnitude to know it's wrong to drink and drive, but it's one that's made thousands of times every year... every day!

If you are competent enough to know right from wrong, then you have all of the tools you need to avoid making a great many mistakes in life. All it takes is a conscious effort to think about what you're doing, why you're doing it, and what could be the outcome or consequences of your actions. When you can commit yourself to doing this, you will find yourself feeling on top of the world. When you actually take the time, no … when you go about making the time to pause and think about the consequences of your actions and then act accordingly, you will appear to have psychic abilities. You will be like a man or woman successfully navigating a minefield blindfolded, for life is nothing but a field of landmines that we have to navigate through.

The funny thing about it is those who just go walking along all willy-nilly as if they don't have a care in the world are the ones who go through that minefield blindfolded and step on one landmine after the other—and in many cases, one mistake might be all you're going to be able to get. That reminds me of a joke I once heard where the comedian said something along the lines of a person gets two chances to steal in the Middle East. After the second time you get caught stealing, the only things you'll be able to steal from that point forward are doughnuts. When you make the effort to think about what could possibly happen if you make this choice or that choice or base what moves you will make on the successes and setbacks you have observed by others' courses of action, you are in fact discovering landmines and bypassing them.

So, as you progress on your journey and you determine what your purpose is, know that life is going to give however much you ask of it, provided you are willing to prove you deserve it. This is how you go about learning that if what you want is worth having, it's not going to come easy. The obstacles you will face are designed to test both your desire and your will. The bubble busters you will encounter exist for that same purpose. However, once you take that first step and keep on stepping, if you keep your eyes on the prize and continue working toward your goal,

God will see to it that your goal is going to be working its way towards you.

In the end, when you develop the habit of making such a conscious effort with everything you do, write, and say, you also develop an almost Jedi-like quality where you appear to be able to successfully navigate the minefield of life blindfolded, and if being able to successfully navigate a minefield blindfolded is neither a gift from God or a baby miracle, I don't know what is!

# SECTION TWO:
# GET SET...

## Lesson One: The Truth About Lies

***I'm not upset that you lied to me, I'm upset that from now on I can't believe you.***
***—Friedrich Nietzsche***

The truth about lies is that—as rare as the situation may be—lies are sometimes necessary; however, just as you cannot use a Band Aid to cure a gunshot wound, one should understand that a lie is only a temporary fix at best. Like Abraham Lincoln said, "You can fool some of the people all of the time, and all of the people some of the time, but you cannot fool all of the people all of the time." There's another old saying, "An honest man has no need for a good memory, and no man is smart enough to remember everything he knows."

I think that might have been Abraham Lincoln too. Ever since I heard those sayings, I have tried to make use of them as a couple of my life's many mantras. What they mean, in short, is that when you tell a lie you will have to remember that lie because, as I said earlier, lies are only a temporary fix at best—so sooner or later that lie will deteriorate and will have to either be reinforced or replaced altogether by another lie ... and another and another. The best one could hope for is that if the lie is told long enough and with enough conviction, not only will people eventually accept it as the truth—you will too.

***A lie may take care of the present, but it has no future. —Unknown***

***A truth that's told with bad intent beats all the lies you can invent. —William Blake***

When I met my wife, Taria, I was already dating another young lady. Although I cared for her very much, I knew in my heart that we were not meant to be together. The truth of the matter was that I was passively looking for someone new to be with. I was in a "bird in the hand beats two in the bush" situation where I was with someone I liked and cared about, but if I could find that certain "something" that was missing from what I had, I would be on that next train. That train came in the day I met Taria, and the timing could not have been any more perfect as my then girlfriend was out of the country at the time. Every day of the week she was gone I had spent with Taria getting to know her, and the more I got to know her, the more I wanted to stay with her. As the week came to an end and my then-girlfriend's return was imminent, I had a decision to make. I no longer had "a bird in the hand." I now had the "two in the bush!"

My then-girlfriend lived about twenty minutes north of me and Taria lived twenty minutes south of me, so there was no chance of running into either one of them while I was with the other, and they both knew that unannounced visits were unacceptable, so I did not have to worry about either of them coming over while the other was with me. I realized I could really have the best of both worlds if I wanted to, but the fact of the matter was I really did care for my then girlfriend, but I was beginning to have feelings for Taria. So, when my then girlfriend returned home, I broke up with her.

Additionally, I did not lie about why I was breaking up with her. I told her I had met someone while she was gone and would be lying if I were to say I did not want to pursue the possibilities. I also told her I would rather have her hate me for having told her the truth as opposed to loving me under a lie. Since I was in full "honest Abe" mode, I also told Taria that I had a girlfriend when we met, but I ended that relationship in order to be with her. I told her, "If I have to lose you for telling you the truth, then I never really had you." Was it a gamble? Absolutely, but it was one that paid off—and on top of that, my ex-girlfriend and I are still good friends to this day.

### *The truth brings with it a great measure of absolution, always. —R.D. Laing*

Before I go any further, I want to make one thing perfectly clear. I do not condone dishonesty. I believe it to be deplorable. Have I been dishonest in my life? I have had my moments, as have we all, for none of us are floating around here with wings and halos. Now, I know we do not live in a vacuum, and there will come times when telling the absolute truth might not be the most practical thing to do. Sometimes it may be because of a need to spare someone's feelings. Sometimes it may be for the greater good.

On an individual level, we may encounter many different times when a lie may be necessary; however, that is no excuse to make a hobby (or a career) out of it. The truth may hurt at first, but at least once the truth is out and the pain has begun, the healing also begins. A lie is like a scab. It looks like it's healing, but when pulled back the wound is still there—and the pulling back can hurt half as bad as the original injury.

I encounter people who lie so much they would not know the truth if it was staring at them in the mirror. It is actually illegal to lie to a police officer, but people do it regardless. I remember I stopped a woman because her license plates were expired. She had no driver's license on her, and the name she gave me was false. Additionally, the next two names she gave me were false. I told her I was going to arrest her if she did not stop giving me false information. Faced with the threat of going to jail, she finally gave me her genuine information, at which time I placed her under arrest anyway. (But wait ... you told her that you were going to arrest her if she kept giving you false information, and you arrested her after she gave you the right information. Didn't you lie to her?)

The answer to that question is no, I did not lie to her. I intended to lock her up anyway after the first name she gave me came up false. I merely allowed her to dig herself into a deeper hole and then threw her what she thought was a rope she could use to climb out of that hole. It just so happened that the hole she dug was too deep for her to climb out of. The sad part about it was when I was close to finishing the paperwork I was informed the woman's mother was in the lobby and wanted to speak with me.

Seeing as how I was almost done, and I knew the bail amount the judge had placed on the woman, I decided to meet with the woman and give her that information. When the mother asked me why I arrested her daughter, I told her, "Because your daughter lied to me." The mother, with sincere shock in her eyes, looked at me and asked, "Are you serious?" I told her I was absolutely serious and that her daughter had given me three false identities before telling me who she really was. (Hint: Here comes the sad part.) The mother looked at me and said, "Well, she told you who she was; you didn't really have to lock her up, did you? It's not like she committed a real crime." I told the mother that it is illegal to lie to a police officer, and her daughter broke the law. I told her the bail amount to get her daughter out of jail, and I excused myself.

I was raised to believe that anything you couldn't do or say in front of your parents wasn't worth doing or saying. I realized then that if this is how this woman's mother viewed right and wrong, then the daughter was raised to also have a skewed view of right and wrong, which is why she could blatantly lie to a police officer without blinking. She also learned the consequences for doing so. In life, you are going to encounter dishonest people. There are also going to be times when you may find yourself in positions where you may either have to be or choose to be less than honest. Dishonesty is something you should be prepared to deal with; however, it is not something you should use as part of your foundation in finding your way.

Remember, you took a pledge of allegiance to yourself when you started reading this book. You must be true with yourself and those around you. When your honesty exudes from within, the world sees you as a person of integrity. Just as a recovering addict must start from day one if he or she has a relapse and engages in his or vice, all it takes is one act of indiscretion—be it actual or even perceived—and you risk throwing away your honorable reputation no matter how many years it took to build up.

None of us are perfect, and we all make mistakes and have lapses in judgment, but the truth about lies is that although there may be times when lying can be a necessary evil, it is evil nonetheless, and an honorable person seeks to avoid having to lie at all costs.

## _Lesson Two: Be True To Your Dreams and Goals_

_Nothing in the world can take the place of persistence. Talent will not. Nothing is more common than unsuccessful men with talent. Genius will not. Unrewarded genius is almost a proverb. Education will not. The world is full of educated derelicts. Persistence, determination and hard work makes the difference. —Calvin Coolidge_

Sometime around 1992–1993, I decided I wanted to become a police officer. I set a goal, and I began doing what was required to achieve that goal. I began making the rounds to different agencies and taking the tests. I even traveled outside of my home state of New Jersey and took tests in Maryland and South Carolina. However, like I said earlier, if there is something you set out to do and you really want to do it, the universe is going to make you earn it. Earlier in this book, I told you about a few goals I had set for myself to achieve by my thirtieth birthday.

Well, the universe had me "earning it" for six years. In 2000, those goals were achieved. The funny thing about setting goals is that you have to keep doing it in order to continue improving yourself. Surprisingly, I was in a comfortable place, and I was enjoying my little taste of success. I knew I had to set new goals, but I really just could not think of anything. I knew I could not allow myself to become complacent and I would never let that happen, but at the same time, I also knew I had just accomplished some pretty big things, so my next set of goals could not be small. It was not until early 2006—ironically another six years later—that I finally set some new goals.

Actually, when I left the East Orange Police Department in 2002 for a higher paying job with my present agency, I did set the goal to knock out the debt I had accumulated over the course of my twenties.

Over the course of the following two years, my raises in pay allowed me to do that quite well. In 2006, I decided to "get my money right." So, I started reading books about money. I was reading books about how certain people acquired their wealth and about how they handled their money.

Then I began implementing the things I was reading about into my life and my finances, and I actually saw positive changes begin to take place, and I shared what I learned with my wife and a few of my friends. The books I was reading also opened my eyes to the importance of entrepreneurship and how starting one's own business can lead to both material wealth and self-satisfaction. I knew then that I had to somehow create my own business. But I asked myself often, "What do I have to offer? What service can I provide?" Then a funny thing happened. After my wife took my advice and encouragement and started her own photography business, I realized exactly what my "service" was: motivation. I realized that for years I was always advising and encouraging friends of mine to follow their dreams. I was always talking about the importance of setting goals.

Basically, I was only sharing what I had learned from the books and tapes I had been reading and listening to over the years. I began to think back on how I came to be where I am and realized that I am in a pretty good place with a bright future ahead of me. It was all because I stood up and told the universe, "I am going to be somebody." I began to wrap my mind around the idea that if I could take all that I have learned and use my life's experiences and observations and share my successes and setbacks as proof that success is possible, I would be able to provide a valuable service after all.

After seeing my wife's business take off successfully, and all because I inspired her to turn her hobby into an opportunity to provide a service to others and make her own money away from her nine to five, I decided to become a motivational speaker, and thus I have decided to take a taste of my own medicine and turn my "hobby" of giving advice and encouragement into a provided service. And after six years of achieving my first set of life goals, I had just set new goals! Early in the summer of 2006, I learned I was eligible to take the sergeant's exam.

Such a promotion would provide a major boost on a great many fronts. For one, there would be a significant pay raise. Second, I would hold a supervisory position where I would have other officers working under me. For me, however, other than the boost in salary, the most appealing aspect of becoming a sergeant with my agency was the fact that at that time there were no supervisors who were people of color, and it would be of some historical significance to be the first black supervisor in my agency's entire history. So, with all of those factors added together, I decided to take the exam. These exams are very competitive and must be prepared for.

There are many courses out there that guarantee greater than "just passing scores." Unfortunately, I was unable to afford a study-preparation study course because my finances were geared toward purchasing my first home, but I figured, "Oh well, I'll just buy the books and make the time to study." I totally believe that people make the time for what they deem to be important. The only problem was that in addition to writing this book, I was also in the process of reading about five books all geared toward my personal self-improvement. I figured that taking the sergeant's exam was just a different area of self-improvement and told myself, "I'll just put that on hold until I take and pass that exam," and with that minor affirmation, I put all of those other books on the shelf.

The funny thing about being a cop—and I tell people this all the time—it is nothing like what you see on television. For all of the cop shows on television that glorify the high speed chases, shoot-outs, and fistfights, what they don't show you are the hours of paperwork that go into making sure all of those physical risks that were taken actually secure a conviction and ensure that we don't get sued or worse, indicted, and/or fired. The only time you're going to see a cop walk into a bar and kick everybody's butts and not see him do any paperwork or make even one arrest is when you're watching a Chuck Norris or Steven Segal movie.

There is a lot of paperwork involved in police work. There are a great many things police can do, even take a person's life, but we have to be able to articulate it on paper, and whatever actions are taken must be in accordance with the law. Therefore, we must know the law, and the law is a very dry subject to have to study.

Every time I cracked open one of those legal books, it was like opening a door that said "Welcome to the Desert" on it. I would be good for maybe ten or eleven pages, and then the sandman would start sprinkling "sleepy dust" on my eyes—and it would be the middle of the day! So, I figured I would walk away and do something then come back with fresh eyes later. The only problem is, for the rest of that particular day, I would never go back to those books! Then one day while doing nothing in particular, I began putting things into perspective. Before the sergeant's exam announcement came, I was already studying. I was reading five books simultaneously. I was studying for something more important than a civil service promotional exam.

I was studying for me! Whereas trying to study statutes and case law nearly had me in a coma, the books I was reading were filling my mind with improved confidence, new ideas, and different perspectives, and upon realizing these things, I began to have yet another epiphany. The books for the sergeant's exam were chosen by those administering the exam. Those books were chosen by the state for a state exam. The books I was reading were chosen by me for me. They were chosen because I felt they were the best books I needed to be reading to help me get my rear in gear in creating my company, HRJR Enterprises, which is my vehicle for helping others find excellence in themselves.

If nothing else, this book is the manifesto of HRJR Enterprises. So what gave substance to this "secondary" epiphany was the realization that in reading those law books and other materials for the sergeant's exam, I was studying on how to become just another rung in the ladder, whereas my books were teaching me how to create my own ladder, put myself atop that ladder, and get others to do the same for themselves. So, I decided to forgo taking the sergeant's exam … at least for now. I realized that my heart wasn't in it. I realized that becoming a "boss" in blue just wasn't for me.

*The worst use of time and life is to work hard to climb the ladder of success only to find it's leaning against the wrong building. —Brian Tracy*

I love my career as a patrolman. I get satisfaction out of what I do in my present position. The money I make is great and continues to get better, so in the absence of a need or desire for financial gain and professional satisfaction, what else is there? Well, I'll tell you— personal gratification. I decided that for me, although becoming a sergeant would bring about a great raise in pay and status, I found myself asking, "Why bother?" What was and remains more important to me is that I do what's necessary to succeed but at the same time be able to enjoy my success and be able to face myself and my family. Like I said, as I was writing this book, I was reading five others.

After those books were done, there were five more, so while taking that exam might have been a worthy goal for the next officer, I realized that following that path myself, at least where I was in my life at that time, would have been breaking a cardinal rule that I hold dear: to thy own self be true. I lost focus. Not necessarily in a bad way, but in trying to study for that exam, I deviated from my path. So, I immediately went back to reading and building my foundation. In short, I have learned to stay true to my dreams and goals. Note: I have come to learn and experience a universal constant: when you give, you get. I am studying materials that will make me a better giver, so the better I am able to give, the more the universe will ensure I receive.

Who knows—there are very few absolutes in this world. Perhaps sometime in the future I may get bitten by the ambition bug and then channel my energy toward taking that promotional exam! Should that become a goal of mine, it shall be one I commit to until it is achieved. All it takes is a little F.O.C.U.S. (Follow One Course Until Successful). What is it that you really want to do? Like the Nike slogan goes, "Just Do It"! Don't allow circumstances to hold you back. Don't allow bubble busters to hold you down. Don't allow yourself to become what Zig Ziglar calls a "SNIOP," which is a person who is "Susceptible to the Negative Influence of Other People."

Remember, what you want to be, do, or have is not supposed to come easily. You are supposed to earn it. You are not entitled to achieve your goals just because you want to; you are entitled to achieve your goals because you have proven yourself worthy of having what it is you want. Don't worry about those other people who look like they have more than you do. You don't know what they might have to be doing to get what they have. You might see a young woman at the club or on campus or in the office wearing the latest fashions, and for all you know, she could be a career shoplifter.

For all you know, she could be linked up to people who sell knock-offs that look so real the designers themselves could not tell the difference from a distance. Never mind the guy you see driving a new car every two years. Chances are he's leasing those cars; in which case he owns nothing and has a steady car payment. For the money he spent on driving three new cars, you could own your car. If every two years he's driving a new car, he's paying that "new car" insurance premium every year— which depending on the car could actually go up whereas your insurance premium could very well go down every year.

In five to six years, he's still paying new car notes, while for the same money he's spending you could very well have paid off your car note, bought a new car, and still kept your original car! The only person responsible for your dreams coming true is you. The only person responsible for your dreams not coming true is you. The universe is going to throw obstacles in your path. The universe is going to introduce you to bubble busters at every turn. In the end, the final result is whatever you have brought it out to be.

Short of death, there are two different points in time when your journey comes to an end:

1. When you succeed at reaching your goal.

2. When you quit.

Either way, you are the one choosing your destination. Like the saying goes, "No matter where you go, there you are," and to that I will add if wherever you happen to end up is not where you wanted to be, you only have yourself to thank for it. Let's say you're getting into your car to take a weekend trip, and along the way your car breaks down in a town you've never even heard of let alone been to. Are you going to just throw your hands up in the air, give up, and start looking for a new apartment in that town? Of course not! You're going to get your car fixed and get on your way.

Now that might take two hours, or it might take an entire day, but surely you're either going to get to where you're going or you're going to find a way to get back home. You are not going to come to an obstacle and just set up camp and move in! You might have to change your game plan. You might have to change your tactics but know what it is you want to do and do what you have to do to get it done.

*As we grow up, we learn that even the one person that wasn't supposed to ever let you down probably will. You will have your heart broken probably more than once, and it's harder every time. You'll break hearts too, so remember how it felt when yours was broken. You'll fight with your best friend. You'll blame a new love for things an old one did. You'll cry because time is passing too fast, and you'll eventually lose someone you love. So, take too many pictures, laugh too much, and love like you've never been hurt because every sixty seconds you spend*

*upset is a minute of happiness you'll never get back. Don't be afraid that your life will end, be afraid that it will never begin.*
*—Anonymous*

## Lesson Three As A Man Thinketh …

*For as he thinketh in his heart, so is he.*
*—Proverbs 23:7*

I truly believe God is all-knowing. By holding this belief, I am acknowledging that God already knows what is going to happen to us on our life's journeys long before we even know we are even on a journey. I believe that whatever happens to me—to all of us—is ultimately his will. The kick of it is I also believe God gave us all free will. So, on the one hand we have the laws of God, on the other we have the laws of man, and then we have the free will to decide which, if any, of those laws we are going to follow. So even though God already knows our outcomes, he also knows how we are going to exercise our free will.

The problem is, in our human imperfection, we have virtually little to no idea as to what our outcomes are going to be—and a great many of us go through life acting as though we don't care either.

*Most people operate on autopilot, doing what comes naturally. They get into a comfort zone of average performance, and seldom question their behaviors.*
*—Brian Tracy*

So, since we have the free will to decide what we are going to do and have the free will to do it—or not— what's the other part of the equation? In a word … consequences. There are consequences for everything we do and everything we don't do. A decision is like a pebble or a stone, while life is like a body of water. When you take action on a decision you've made, you are throwing that pebble or stone into that body of water. Now there may be a big splash or a little plop, but either way the impact causes ripples in the water, and depending on the size of the stone, you could very well make ripples that eventually turn into waves.

Decision + Action = Consequence

Decision + Inaction = Consequence

The brain is an extremely powerful muscle. It's the muscle that controls all others. Your fingers move because your brain tells them to. You walk when your brain activates your left foot to move in front of your right foot over and over again. When the body is fatigued nearly to the part of surrender, it's the brain that either allows the body to give in or releases the adrenaline and other chemicals the body may need to press on just a little longer. In short, to a great extent, the body will achieve whatever the mind believes.

Have you ever misplaced something small like your wallet, watch, or TV remote control and torn up the house looking for it only to have your husband, wife, or one of your children come into the room, go over to the dresser, pick up the item, and say, "Here it is right under your nose!" Now, why do you think it is that you could not spot that remote control or your watch? Did you at any point, by chance, say to yourself or to one of your loved ones, "I can't find it"? Be honest, I know I've experienced this, and if you haven't, either you're not being totally honest, or you're just luckily long overdue! The reason we all experienced this strange phenomenon is because we all used that magically poisonous word— can't.

Remember, the body will achieve what the mind believes, and when we all said to ourselves or our loved ones, "I can't find it," our brains sent a message to our eyes instructing them to not see the very things we were looking for. Try this and see if it does not change your perception on the matter. The next time you find yourself looking for something, you will find that your natural response is going to be to say "I can't find it"; however, when you catch yourself saying those words either to yourself or aloud, I want you to immediately stop and correct yourself by telling yourself and those around you, "I am having difficulty finding" whatever item you are looking for.

Next, tell yourself, "I know it's here, and I'm going to find it." I guarantee you'll increase the chances of you being the one who finds whatever it is you are looking for. Why? Well, because of one simple principle—difficulty does not equate to impossibility. When you use a word like can't, you eliminate the chance for possibility.

In short, it is pretty much a guarantee that when you tell yourself you can't do something, you won't. The same dynamic applies to changing your life's situation for the better. When you decide you need to make a change and act on it, you begin the process of manifesting the changes necessary to improve your life. As I stated before, the decision to make a change is a good start to improving your situation, but without taking any action, your decision is both useless and worthless. I say useless because well, how else would you describe something you have no use for?

What use do you have for an idea that you have no intentions of acting upon? Having made a decision you don't plan on acting upon is about as useful as a three-legged horse in the Kentucky Derby. I used the word worthless because the decision you came up with could very well be the foundation to future success on many different levels; however, without taking any action on those decisions to manifest them into reality, there is absolutely no worth in that decision having ever been made. There was a movie that came out in 2004 called Super-Size Me. It was actually a documentary in which the main character ate nothing but McDonald's food for a period of thirty days.

Breakfast, lunch, and dinner were all Mickey D's, and for the whole month he also checked in regularly with a doctor just to see what, if any, effects his diet was having on his body. After thirty days of eating nothing but McDonald's food, he gained twenty-four and a half pounds and experienced mood swings, sexual dysfunction, and severe liver damage. It took him a year and two months to lose the weight it only took him thirty days to gain.

The overall moral of the story is: what one may consider a "treat" is good once in a while, but when you feed your body junk, your body will let you know just how much it does not appreciate it. The same holds true with our brains. Whatever you feed your mind, your body will manifest. Look at a lot of young children and teenagers out there. A great many of them can recite the lyrics to all of the songs whose videos appear on MTV and BET, but take those same kids and ask them to recite a speech by President John F. Kennedy, President Franklin D. Roosevelt, Mohandas Karamchand Gandhi, Dr. Martin Luther King, Jr., or El-Hajj Malik El-Shabazz (more commonly known as Malcolm X), and at best you'll get a catchphrase.

On that same note, there are young people out there who make millions of dollars in the drug trade using all kinds of mathematic principles but would miserably fail a ninth-grade algebra exam, and others who could recite all of the stats of their favorite athletes and the names of all the members of their favorite teams but not be able to tell you who the members are on the city council where they live. Because of music videos, magazines, and all kinds of entertainment programs on television, we are exposed to the lifestyles that many celebrities live.

The good thing that can be derived from this is that by seeing all the toys, flashy cars, hottest clothes, and fancy homes, we can see what the funner things in life are (yes—I said "funner" because surely these are not truly the finer things in life); however, what we do not see is the work that goes into getting those things. Even worse, for those who aren't legitimately working for those things, you don't get to see exactly what they do to be able to have that kind of lifestyle.

***For what is a man profited, if he shall gain the whole world, and lose his own soul?***
***—Matthew 16:26***

I wouldn't mind driving a high performance car, taking foreign vacations, having tailor-made suits, and a big mansion—but not at the expense of my integrity, and certainly not at the expense of my soul. You can be, do, and have anything you want as long as you're willing to do what is required in order to achieve it. If you're reading this book, then surely you are only concerned with legitimate achievement; however, if you're thinking you're going to find quick-fix solutions, then I am afraid you picked up the wrong book. All you have to do is say what it is you want to do. That is the beginning. When I set out to become a motivational speaker, the first question I asked myself was, "What are you going to say?" Then I realized I had taken notes from many of the books that I have read.

I had jotted down many of my opinions and thoughts in the form of blogs on the Internet. It turned out I had plenty to say! I knew I could "talk good," but I wanted to be able to "speak well," so I did some research and found out about Toastmasters International®, an organization created to help people improve their communication and leadership skills. I joined a local chapter, and my training began. I also sent a letter to my grade school principal asking her if I could address the school's graduating class at its commencement ceremony, which she graciously obliged.

I appeared at the ceremony expecting to be one of the speakers present. It turned out I was to be the keynote speaker. I delivered a twenty-minute speech, and although I specifically asked to not be paid, there was $150 in cash inside of the thank you card her secretary gave me at the conclusion of the ceremony. Not only had I become a speaker, I had become a paid speaker. Not too shabby for my first time out, huh?

### *For as he thinketh in his heart, so is he.*
### *—Proverbs 23:7*

After hearing a few of my speeches at my local Toastmasters club meetings and reading some of my blogs, one of my mentors suggested I write a book. I don't remember exactly when I made the decision to put this book together, but when I did make that decision, everything started falling into place. In fact, many of my first speech assignments in Toastmasters are lessons that are in this book! I made the decision I was going to become a police officer, and I became one. I made the decision I was going to become a speaker, and I became one. I made the decision to become an author, and even if you and I are the only ones to ever read this book, I still became an author.

### *SIMS … The Game of Life*

Have you ever heard of a game called "the Sims"? My wife, her mother, her sister, and even our eight-year old niece are all hooked on this game. This is a game where you get to not only create buildings and entire communities, but you can also create the people that live in these communities, and you set them on their merry ways. However, these characters do not have free will. You can set them on a particular course, but after a while you have to change their activities or else they'll get sick or even lose their jobs—jobs you give them. To some small degree, the person playing this game can easily make the mistake that they are playing God. However, this is the real world; this is life, and in life there is no "replay" button. We can't just push "pause" on our lives and come back and play later. I think God is sitting in a nice cushy recliner with a remote control, watching us all on a world-sized flat screen plasma television, and we mere mortals are like one big game of "the Sims." But here's the kicker— even though God gave us the free will to choose what we're going to do, God already knows the outcome of whatever choice we decide to make.

I want you to remember one thing: God alone has the power to show you who is God. It is my personal belief that our paths have already been predetermined. It is also my personal belief, based on a great many of my personal experiences, that God has an incredible sense of humor. In the end, it's good to decide that you need to make a change in your life, but once you've made that decision, you need to decide exactly what changes need to be made, create strategies to implement those changes, then follow through on those strategies.

There is absolutely no reason why you cannot be whatever it is you want to be. You can do or have whatever you want. The only real problems that exist are, if you cannot accept the fact that it's not going to come just because you want it, it's not going to come easy, and even though you may give yourself a time limit to achieve your goal, that is only a guideline for you because the universe could care less about when you want to achieve your goal. If what you want is truly meant to be yours, then the universe will see to it that you get it, but only when you have proven yourself worthy, and not a day sooner. So, dream big!

Decide who or what you want to be then set out to be that person. Before closing this lesson, I want to tell you about one young man's story. Since he was a teenager he knew he wanted to direct movies. After a tour on a movie lot, he just set out to be a movie director, but during the course of the tour, he wasn't where the real action was—the sound stages—so he snuck off to find them on his own. He even met and spoke with a studio executive who expressed an interest in his ideas. The next day he put on a suit, took his father's briefcase (loaded only with his lunch), and walked onto that studio lot right through the front gate and past the guardhouse like he belonged there.

He found an abandoned trailer and put his name on the door followed by the word Director. He spent the summer meeting writers, directors, and just about everyone involved in the movie-making process. Three years later, after having become a regular face on the lot, he showed a studio executive a short film he put together and was offered a seven-year contract to direct a television series. His name: Steven Spielberg.

## Lesson Four: Self-Pride

### No one has a greater asset for his business than a man's pride in his work. —Hosea Ballou

What ever happened to the belief in "a job well done is its own reward"? Why is it that people expect to be rewarded for everything they do—even things they are supposed to be doing? Why is it that one feels he must be praised in order to feel that he has done well? What is more important: the praise one gets after he has done well, or the wisdom gained along the way while achieving a goal? After all the praise has died down and faded away, what is there left? All that is left is the memory of what was done right and what was done wrong. When one goes about moving on to the next task or goal and he has learned to use what was done right and discard what was done wrong, regardless of the outcome, that is the gaining of wisdom. With accomplishing every task, with every journey, you learn things along the way. You learn what works and what does not.

### Every job is a self-portrait of the person who does it. Autograph your work with excellence. —Unknown

The most significant experience in my life that taught me the value of self-pride was when I was in boot camp for the Air Force. When my flight screwed up we caught grief, and when we did good we caught grief! The only time we got a congratulatory word from the drill instructors was when we graduated—and I think it was because they knew they did a good job! Now, I don't know about the rest of the guys in my flight, but what I learned from that experience was that we knew when we did a good job, regardless of whether or not we got kudos for it. After all, drill instructors are not in the business of giving pats on the head for a job well done.

They are in the business of "drilling" duty and discipline into our heads because someday we could be faced with a life and death situation, and all we would have to fall back on is our training and our discipline. I learned that when we did the job right they knew we did the job right, but to praise us would make us complacent, even lazy perhaps. Instead, they gave us hell, and we continued to work harder and harder, and the praise came at graduation—when the whole mission was accomplished. When I was in boot camp, I really began to learn the meaning of "a journey of a thousand miles." It was actually six weeks, but as much as we marched, we probably did cover over a thousand miles!

There was day one, and then forty-two "day ones" later, it was over; however, I learned a lot about myself during those forty-two days. I was nineteen years old, and I had put myself in a position where my comfort zone was just under two thousand miles away. For the following six weeks, I held the title of "dorm chief." In the chain of command, I fell into place right under the drill instructor. I had a staff of four squad leaders, who in turn each had about ten to twelve men under them to make up our whole formation, or "flight," as we were called. At nineteen years old, I was one of the youngest men there, but I was in charge of everyone.

This was, and remains to be, one of the most humbling experiences of my life. There were men in my flight who had wives and kids back home, and here they were being ordered around by a nineteen-year-old kid who had never really been anywhere and who had never really done anything. I had never been that far away from home, and I was not only scared of failure on a daily basis, I was scared of the consequences for failing! Every section of the barracks had two dormitories with one flight in each dorm, and both flights started training on the same night. Oh yes, I said night. You see, no matter what time you may have left home that morning, if your destination was Lackland Air Force Base with orders in hand for basic military training, you arrived in San Antonio at night! What better time for the mind games to begin than in the hours of darkness?

After assigning the recruits to their respective flights and dormitories, or "bays," the drill instructors would pit the two flights against each other in order to instill pride and loyalty within the flights. Not only were we evaluated on our individual progress and our progress as a flight, but our progress was also evaluated against that of the other flight. During the fourth week of training, my flight competed with the other flight in everything from cleaning our dorms, to our appearance, to marching and drill—everything. The flight that came out on top would be given the title "Honor Flight," and with that distinction came a lot of perks. You'd be surprised at how exciting being able to make a telephone call, eat a candy bar, or going to Burger King is!

However, I told my guys, "Let's not do this for Honor Flight. Let's do this because it has to be done anyway." I would go on to explain that after the first couple of times of having to repeat work where we tried to take shortcuts, we learned that anything worth doing was worth doing right the first time, so "let's just make sure that whatever we do, we put in the work required for it to be done right the first time." Every time someone took a shortcut thinking he won't find this, or they won't look for that, whatever it was, the drill instructor would go straight to it or spot the shortcut immediately.

So early on we agreed as a unit ... no shortcuts. In the end, we won the title of Honor Flight, and all of those extra little perks and privileges that came along with it. As dorm chief, I was awarded a special certificate of recognition at our graduation ceremony. This had been the hardest thing I had ever done in my life, and I came out of it on top, and I knew it in my heart! Praise is good. It is good to be recognized for having done something well or for having done something that was the right thing to do; however, it should mean more to the one who did it. When you have done well and you can look at yourself in the mirror and say, "I did good," then even if no one else says it, you know, and that should be all that matters. It doesn't matter what it is you're doing; if it is something you are supposed to be doing, you should not be expecting any special accolades.

When my parents divorced, I was about three or four years old. Primarily I lived with my mother until the age of ten. She got a job offer in Chicago, and between her and my father, it was decided that I would remain in New Jersey and stay with my father. Other than on Father's Day, he never got any special rewards for being there for me, nor did he look or ask for any. He was doing what a man was supposed to do: raise his son to be a good person. If a police officer or a firefighter gets hurt or worse on the job while saving someone else's life, you will have some people who will say, "They're heroes, gifts to us from God," while you'll have others who will say, "Well, that's what they get paid for."

Now, as cynical and uncaring as that may sound, it also happens to be the truth. There are no ticker tape parades after an arrest is made or after a fire has been put out. You do the job, and if you don't get so much as a "thank you," even if you put out your best effort or more, knowing within yourself that you put it all on the line is what you should take pride in. When you set the goal to do something well or do something because it is the right thing to do, once you have succeeded, then you are the first to be rewarded. Not with accolades, money, or some other tangible object. Pride is the reward. When a person would rather have someone else be proud of him than him having pride in himself, he will rarely find it, and thus he is lost.

*The biggest mistake we could make in our lives is thinking that we work for anybody but ourselves.*
*—Brian Tracy*

There are other "self" words that tie into this lesson. Such words are self-respect and self-esteem. Nonetheless, the operative word here is self. Be it your sense of pride, respect, or esteem, it all starts from within. Surely if "charity begins in the home," so does your sense of pride, respect, and esteem. Your foundation for these things rests within yourself. This reminds me of an episode of The Cosby Show where one of the kids had a science project to do. She waited until pretty much the last minute to put her project together, and then when the day came to present the project, she saw that her friends had really gone all out on theirs—one kid had a working volcano, another had a self-contained hurricane, and yet another had an experiment in robotics.

What did the Cosby kid have? A mobile of the solar system consisting of some painted Styrofoam balls, wire, and string. She did not do well in that project and in the end knew that she could have and should have done better. If you have no pride in what you do, it will show; no one will care to recognize poor effort, and you will not excel. How do you allow people to address you?

Personally, I refuse to allow anyone to address me in a demeaning or disrespectful manner. I do not incite an argument, but I do politely make it known that there is such a way in which I will not be spoken to. In my line of work as a police officer, I have encountered individuals whose attitude can best be described as "salty," and I have had other coworkers say to me, "That's just how he is." I made it known that I didn't care if the president of the United States allowed himself to be spoken to that way—it is unacceptable when addressing me. If you lack respect for yourself, be it in terms of how you present yourself or how you allow yourself to be treated, then no one else shall respect you. My father and I have a great relationship. Although there was never a question as to who was the adult and who was the child, he was also very much a big brother along with being a father.

And like brothers are prone to do, we joked around with one another a lot. However, as I grew older, I had begun noticing that my father would always make me the butt of his jokes when we were around others. Also, as I grew into adulthood, I could get a little sharper with my wit than I could as a child. Now, it just so happens that we are both members of the same fraternal organization, so in a sense, my father is my brother, and when we would get around other brothers, he would lay into me heavy! At first I would not go back with the same sting as I would when we would be joking between ourselves because I was being the respectful son; however, there was one particular day when I had reached my wit's end. My then-girlfriend, Taria, and I had been dating for a couple of months, and we were all at a cookout being thrown by our brothers in New York. My father was in rare form. He was digging into me over just about anything I did, and the other brothers were laughing. Now, the problem I had with that was that although the brothers were laughing with him, they were laughing at me, and that was unacceptable.

Additionally, Taria was there seeing me get clowned, and no woman wants to be with a man who cannot stand up for himself. So, I started first off by telling my father to "shut up." That threw him back! Then I turned the tables and started digging into him with a few stingers of my own; then Taria and I went off to another area of the cookout. This was not about disrespecting my father. This was about standing my ground in an equal arena, i.e. "the brotherhood," and how I would and would not allow myself to be both treated and viewed by others.

Later that night, my father called me demanding that I show him more respect when we were out in public. I said, "Dad, I love you, but you need to check yourself. When we joke with one another, that's one thing, but you always have to make me the butt of your jokes around the brothers, and I'm tired of it. And today you were doing it not only in front of them, but in front of my woman too!

Now if these people look at you treating me like this, they're going to go back to wherever and say, 'His pops has no respect for him,' and if they see or believe that my own father doesn't even respect me, then they are going to wonder why should they bother to respect me?" After having said that, he saw it for what it was, and he apologized. Since then, he still jokes on me, and I with him—but it's all in fun, and it doesn't bear the same sting as before. Yet again, he saw that his boy was becoming a man who would be strong enough to stand up for himself—even against him! This leads me to my next question. Do you have a problem asserting yourself when you know and believe in your heart you are right? You must be willing to stand up for yourself.

Remember, you've been a fighter since before you were born. You beat out five hundred million other sperm just to be here, so why let all of that effort go to waste? You must have enough love for and faith in yourself to be able to stand up for yourself. Never mind the bully in the playground or the annoying supervisor at work; there is no bigger bully than the universe itself, and when you can find the fortitude in your heart to stand up against the universe for your rightful place in it, in time you will find that instead of you having to stand up against the universe, the universe will be standing up for you!

In the end, you must know in your heart that you are doing the right thing. When you shine a flashlight against a wall, the light stops right there, but what happens when you shine a flashlight into a mirror? The light reflects and bounces right back. Life works the same way. However, you envision yourself as the battery, and your conduct is the light bulb. Life is the mirror, and however you project your conduct, the world shall reflect the same upon you.

One of the most fundamental laws you have to acknowledge and live by when dealing with self-pride is the hardest time to do the right thing is to do it when there is no one around—when there may be no one around to see what you have done, thus no one around to pat you on the head. However, if you have pride in yourself and your number one goal is to succeed for the sake of succeeding or to do what is right because it is the right thing to do, once you have succeeded, should you not be praised, it will not matter, and should you be showered with praise or other more tangible accolades, well, that is just the icing on the cake!

## Lesson Five: The Art of Doing Right by Being Right

*When you do everything right, there are rewards. When you do everything wrong, there are consequences. —Dr. Larry Pannell, Band Director Grambling State University*

This lesson is going to be one that stands on its own merit. The two most powerful words in the English language are I am. When you have embraced these words and incorporated them into your life, you have begun the art of being. Ultimately, what I want you to take from this lesson is that if you're going to be successful in life, you're going to have to do the right things. The only way you're ever going to know that you are doing the right things is by learning from having done the wrong things. This is how you gain wisdom.

When you learn how to do something right, the more you do it, the more you become it. In the late nineties, I came to a realization about myself and my family. I come from proud people. I come from people who don't want to be right about everything—they have to be right about everything. My grandmother was a woman who you listened to whether you wanted to or not. If it was not her way, it was not the way.

My family never claimed to be perfect or to know everything, but if you want to contest a point with a member of my family, you had better know your stuff. Growing up, it was difficult being around people who just had to be right about everything, but as I fumbled through adolescence and tripped into adulthood, I began to learn that my family was the way it was not because they needed to be right, it was just that my family always believed in what was right.

Now, I'm not ultra-religious, but I was raised in the Baptist church and educated in the Catholic school system. With that said, I guess the best way to describe my family's belief in what is right is with the following scripture:

*No weapon that is formed against thee shall prosper; and every tongue that shall rise against thee in judgment thou shalt condemn. This is the heritage of the servants of the Lord, and their righteousness is of me, saith the Lord.*
*—Isaiah 54:17*

What I began to learn for myself is that another way to look at my family was in such a way where we believe that if we have God on our side, who can stand against us? This is the same foundation in faith that gave Japanese fighter pilots the courage to fly their planes into ships; the same foundation in faith that gave students the courage to lay their bodies down in front of tanks in Tiananmen Square, China; and the same foundation in faith that people in the Middle East and Africa have when they fight tanks with sticks and stones. Ask yourself, who should you fear most: the operator of the tank who can blow you away with the push of a button or the person who is willing to go against that tank with only a club or stone in hand?

Personally, I have made many mistakes in my life. Some were made out of arrogance, and some were made out of ignorance. However, as I matured, I began to learn from my mistakes, and instead of repeating them, I would make new ones to learn from. Every experience became a file for me to store in my databank of dumb decisions. In my studies and experiences, I learned that in order to really begin learning from the mistakes I made I needed to be the first one to acknowledge that I had made a mistake and that if it was brought to my attention that I had in fact made a mistake, not to hesitate to apologize for it and attempt to make amends, and I began to consciously live my life this way.

Throughout my life, there were minor mistakes I have made, and then there were a couple whoppers, I mean mistakes that I spent years beating myself up over. However, I learned to face myself, and then I learned to forgive myself. When I made those distinctions in my life, I became stronger. It was then that I truly became a man. Like I said earlier, my father is one who will not allow you to forget the mistakes you've made.

There was one situation where I cannot remember exactly what I had done that he was reminding me that I did, but I do remember saying to him, "Yeah, okay, I made that mistake. I did that … but I know I messed up, and I don't plan on doing it again, so leave it alone." Since I can't remember what mistake it was I had made, and since he obviously did leave it alone, I guess I haven't repeated that mistake!

You see, there are people out there in the world who love to point the finger of blame, but like the old saying goes, "When you point the finger of blame, there are three fingers pointing back at you." I learned to be the one who held me accountable to myself before anyone else could. I learned that if I thought about the consequences of my actions before I actually acted out, I would be better off. To this date, I have been. I also learned that the majority of people out there do not take the time to think about the consequences of their actions.

What is truly sad, however, is that when someone is brought to face their misdeeds or mistakes, instead of saying, "I was wrong," they look to place the blame or fault somewhere else—anywhere else rather than where it actually belongs.

If a person gets pulled over and gets a ticket for speeding, she doesn't accept responsibility; she gets mad because she was the one who got caught and not the two or three cars that were in front of her. As a police officer, I am more inclined to show some discretion and give a break to someone who says, "I'm sorry, officer. I know I was speeding," as opposed to someone who asks me, "Is there a problem?" or "You wanna tell me why you stopped me?" when they know good and well why they were stopped.

*A man may fall many times, but he won't be a failure until he says someone pushed him.*
*—Elmer G. Letterman*

I believe one of the main reasons so many people in the world do not do as well as they wish is because of a tremendous lack of self-accountability. People don't want to take responsibility for their actions and decisions. People spend a lifetime eating fast food then want to sue the fast food chain because they're obese. People spend a lifetime smoking, and when they develop cancer, their families want to sue the tobacco companies.

You always want to protect the ones you love most, and who do people love better than themselves? So, it's easier to blame someone, anyone else, rather than accept responsibility for yourself, but in the end, you will be the one who always suffers most for it. On the way to achieving your goals, you're going to make mistakes, but if you do not acknowledge them and learn from them, you're not really going to grow and become better.

Additionally, the only way you will be able to find a way is by occasionally going the wrong way. It's been said that those who are successful became so by doing the right things, but they learned all of the right things from having done the wrong things. Ultimately, if you want more for yourself, you're going to have to assume accountability for yourself. When you do, you become stronger. When you do, you make it even harder for other people to bust your bubble. There are always going to be people out there who look for the worst in a situation, some because they just don't know any better. I have learned that I cannot save the world, and I cannot hold myself accountable for what other people think or do. I can only hold myself accountable for what I do.

I can only blame myself for the mistakes I make, and the same goes for you. When you reach a point within your life (and I hope you reach that point while reading this book) where you become your toughest critic, you will be like the character Neo in the movie The Matrix after he swallowed the red pill and began to see the world for what it really was. I am guaranteeing you that when you begin to take stock in yourself and hold yourself accountable for what you do instead of blaming others you will find yourself living a life of freedom like you never knew before.

In the movie The Matrix, "the matrix" was what we thought the world was; even better, it was what we were programmed to believe it was. The people in the matrix went about their day-to-day lives just reacting to whatever happened to them, when in "reality" the world was a wasteland run by supercomputers that used human beings as living batteries.

There was a small contingent of human beings who were "unplugged" from the matrix and lived in a place called Zion, and they had the means to enter and exit the matrix at will. The benefit they had over others in the matrix was that because their minds were "opened" to their true reality, and thus they knew that the matrix was a prefabricated world where certain laws of physics could be broken because, after all, none of it was real, they appeared to possess superhuman abilities. Actually, a better way to describe it would be to say that life in the matrix was as real as one's mind allowed it to be.

There was a scene in the movie that really stuck with me. Neo, the hero of the movie, was speaking to a small child who was levitating objects in the room they were in and also bending spoons. When he asked the child how was he able to bend the spoons, the child told him that it was easy to bend the spoon "because there was no spoon." As the movie went on, Neo learned that he could do amazing things, and the more he believed in what he could do within the matrix, the more powerful he became—up to actually being able to exert his power "outside" of the matrix.

When you reach a level of self-clarity where you act only after evaluating your actions based on taking the consequences of your actions into consideration and then holding yourself accountable to your shortcomings, you shall reach a similar level of clarity and freedom. Naturally, I am not saying you'll be able to fly, stop bullets, or do that funky lean-back-bullet-dodging maneuver, but like the people of Zion, you will be among a very select few who see the world for how it really is and the people in it for whom they really are, and this is where your power will come from.

As you can tell by now, I love to watch movies. Depending on how good the movie is, it can really be hard to tell if art is imitating life or if life is imitating art. Before concluding on this point, I want you to just bear with me for one more movie quote that will drive this point home. In the movie Blade, there is a scene where Wesley Snipes—who plays the lead character, a vampire hunter— and a female doctor who was bitten by a vampire the night before are hunting a human slave called a "familiar." When she asks him how he knows where the "familiar" is going to be, he responds, "When you know the nature of a thing, you know what it's capable of." It has been my experience that with good observational skills, both internal and external, you can manipulate what people do and how they do it. You can even manipulate them into doing things they probably would not want to do if it came down to leaving them to themselves.

Advertising and marketing companies make millions doing this every year! It is my hope that upon gaining this freedom and clarity of thought, you would use your newly found skills for good and not evil. To repeat the quote at the beginning of this section, "When you do everything right, there are rewards. When you do everything wrong, there are consequences."

### _Lesson Six: The Power of Being Bigger than You Are_

### _Fake it until you make it! —Unknown_

A few years ago, Chris Rock and the late Bernie Mac starred in a movie called Head of State where Chris Rock played a low-level local politician who was picked by some Washington big wigs to run for president of the United States, but unbeknownst to Rock's character, they picked him to lose. Bernie Mac played Rock's older brother whom Rock called on for support and advice. There was a scene in the movie where Bernie Mac was trying to get Rock to pay closer attention to the image he was portraying, and the piece of advice he gave him has stuck with me ever since.

What he said was, "You have to dress for the job you want, not for the job you already got." This piece of advice is profound as far as I'm concerned. You see, you can't become more than what you already are by doing nothing. You may age, but you surely won't grow. One of the most important lessons I have learned during my personal journey through life is that if you want to keep on getting what you're getting, keep on doing what you're doing. Another thing people need to realize is that the world does not owe them success. The only thing the world has to give you is a planet to live on and air to breathe. As for the quality of your life while you're here, well, that's up to you!

I became a police officer in 2000, and as I have told you already, before I became a police officer, I was a loss prevention agent for Old Navy. Basically, I was chasing down shoplifters and catching dishonest employees who were either stealing for themselves or giving their friends free merchandise or unauthorized "discounts." I went from making $20K–$21K a year to a salary based on $22K a year while I was in the police academy. The day I graduated from the academy, my salary jumped up to $39K a year. After two years, I went to my present agency where my starting salary was just over $60K a year. Four years after that, and for the first time in my life, I made over $100K for the year! Did this come to pass because I was some kind of super-cop who could demand his own salary? I wish, but no.

In a nutshell, my raise in salary was a culmination of determination, networking, and a whole lot of luck! Now despite my drive, people skills, and having fallen under a lucky star, there were other cops at my original department who could have easily taken that job from me on the sheer basis of just having more experience than me.

### *Luck is what happens when preparation meets opportunity. —Darrell K. Royal*

When I left my old job, I was not quite at the lowest tier of the pay scale, and I was far from the top. However, when I started at my new job, my starting salary was more than what my former sergeant's salary was, and four years later, my salary as a patrolman was probably equal to that of a lieutenant's salary at my old job. Now, my old department is more or less "inner city." Not quite the Bronx, New York, but not Saddle River, New Jersey, either. The officers at my old job stay rocking and rolling every day, and quite frankly, they deserve far more than what they are getting paid, and they know this; however, there are those that choose to stay there.

For the life of me, I still cannot understand that mentality. I understand "staying in the hood" and working for "the people"; however, in a job where any day you kiss your family good-bye could be your last, you would think that people would expect, even demand, that they be fairly compensated. After all, when put into the context that you could be killed on the job, your salary does bear some reflection on how much your employer thinks your life is worth. Personally, my life is priceless, but since no employer is going to pay that amount, I felt we had to come to some kind of reasonable compromise! Earlier in my life I saw that there was more to the world than my hometown, and I wanted to see some of it and have a part of it.

My hometown was my "box," and in order for me to succeed, I knew I had to go outside that box, and go outside that box is exactly what I did. Imagine being in a cell. Now imagine that all four walls to the cell are made of glass—glass that's so clean you can't even see your reflection in it. All day, every day, and every night too, you can see everything that's going on outside your cell, and everything you see looks good. Now, inside your cell you are sheltered and fed, but the people outside your cell are living and eating far better than you are. After a few years the walls to that cell begin to deteriorate down to the point where they are no longer there. Now those walls are gone, and you are free to go about living that good life you have been looking at all those years ... but you don't. You can even reach out and feel that those walls are no longer there, but you stay in your cell.

It's all about comfort and fear, pain and pleasure. People fear leaving their comfort zones. After achieving a little piece of success, they become comfortable. After a while, that comfort turns into complacency. Complacency is what you have when you either forget or ignore the struggle you once endured to get to where you are. It takes determination and hard work to achieve any significant measure of success. However, work is about struggle, and struggle is about pain.

Pain is what everyone wishes to avoid, so for some it is easier, if not pleasurable, to accept where they are, despite the fact they have the same options available to them as those who are living the life they are looking at and even want. Unfortunately, what most people fail to realize is that pleasure is the reward for enduring the pain of the struggle. People just want pleasure without earning it. Some get it that way, but surely it is short-lived.

*If there is no struggle there is no progress. Those who profess to favor freedom and yet deprecate agitation, are men who want crops without plowing the ground, they want rain without thunder and lightning. They want the ocean without the awful roar of its many waters. This struggle may be a moral one, or it may be a physical one, and it may be both moral and physical, but it must be a struggle. Power concedes nothing without a demand. It never did and it never will.*

*—Frederick Douglass, West India Emancipation Speech, Aug. 4, 1856*

There is a commonly known saying: "Fake it till you make it." Now, I don't particularly subscribe to "faking" in the sense of being fraudulent, but just like the Bernie Mac quote earlier, I think what the saying means is that people can either see you as who/how you used to be, who/how you are, or who/how you will soon be; ultimately, how you present and carry yourself will be the gauge by which you will be measured. You see, when you believe in your goals and dreams to the point where you can visualize yourself as having already fulfilled them, you begin to set the achieving of your goals into motion.

The next thing you should be doing is carrying yourself as though you already have achieved your goals. You might be driving a Hyundai, but if you've set forth towards getting that Mercedes Benz, until you actually have that Benz, treat your Hyundai as you would that Benz. People will see you carrying yourself differently. They'll see you walking differently. You might even be talking differently, and they might not understand. That's okay! They don't have to understand until you're ready for them to—or until you've made it obvious. For example, when you've moved out of your parents' house or your apartment into a house of your own, and you've turned that Hyundai into a Benz. Then they'll get it! When it comes to achieving your goals, you have to be your biggest cheerleader. No one understands your vision better than you.

The fire does not burn in anyone else's belly hotter than it burns in yours; however, the one thing you have in your favor is the overwhelming human need for belonging and belief in what is good. Even if it wasn't their idea, people want to belong to something they believe in, especially if it's something they feel they can benefit from. So, you've visualized yourself having already achieved your goal. It's one thing to have that mansion in your mind, but in order to manifest it into your life, you will have to find a way to get the right people into your life who can help you along the way.

When you reach the point where you can convey your goals and dreams to others and get them to see them as vividly as you do, you're going to begin to create momentum. Momentum is an extremely necessary ingredient while on the road to achieving your goals. When this book was nothing more than a very long and well-written essay, I shared my vision with a select group of people who I knew would both support the big picture and also provide me with the proper grounding when needed in case my head ever got too big. The stronger you believe in yourself and the harder you fight to overcome whatever obstacles are thrown your way just goes to increase your momentum. You will also begin to discover that the more you put yourself out there, the more resources and connections will be made available to you.

They will be magnetically drawn to you. The funny thing about building up your momentum is that it can help you or hurt you. You might not be where you want to be, but if you are actively working toward your goal, there's nothing stopping you from talking yourself up. Remember—you are your biggest cheerleader. Just as the universe is always watching, people are always listening. They either want to see you win or see you fall flat on your face. So, if you're looking to talk yourself up but not actually follow through, be careful. It's one thing to fake it till you make it, but it's something totally different to just live a lie. You can build up momentum that you can ride all the way to the successful completion of your goals, or you can build up the unhealthy kind of momentum than can overwhelm you and take you someplace you may not want to end up.

The first place wherein which you become anything is in your heart. If in your heart you believe you are going to be a singer, actor, athlete, teacher, plumber, astronaut, whatever, then you are already that thing. All that remains is that you learn the skills necessary to successfully be that thing. When I made the decision to become a motivational speaker, I don't ever recall having said, "I'm going to be a motivational speaker." Even when I joined Toastmasters, at my very first meeting I remember telling the members, "I have decided to be a motivational speaker, and I am here to become great at it." I had people in my life question and doubt me. After I self-published and released the first copies of this book back in 2007, someone on my job put a photocopy of my book's cover upon the bulletin board in a spot that's normally reserved for someone being joked on or made fun of.

Normally it's harmless humor, but I knew it was different for me. It was different because there wasn't anything funny about what I was doing. I set out to write a book, and I was being ridiculed for it. However, just by the very nature of you having this book in your hands, it is clear I am having the last laugh. Most people never find their way because they fear rejection and ridicule.

Everyone has dreams. Everyone has a moment when they see themselves wanting, being, and having more in their lives. What separates them from those considered successful is the level of belief in their hearts and the level of commitment in their deeds. It does not take much to be whatever it is you want to be. Not if it is important enough. Remember, that is the point of this book. If something is important enough to you, you will find a way to make a way! In the book Rich Dad, Poor Dad, Robert Kiyosaki tells us that one of the secrets of the rich is that they spend more time asking of themselves what they can do than telling themselves what they can't do.

People are what they are because they have made the decision to be so. If you're a high school athlete who wants to get into a Division I college or university, you're going to play like you're already there. If you're a college athlete who wants to play in the professional leagues, you're going to play like you're already there. The universe is like God's talent scout. It's always watching. My mother always says, "You play like you practice." Many of my life's experiences have proven this to be true time and time again. If you practice hard, you'll play hard. If you practice to win, you'll play to win. If you practice being bigger than you are, someday you will be bigger than you are.

In 2006, I changed the outgoing message on my cellular phone. Instead of hearing, "Hey, this is Harold," people hear, "Hello. You've reached Harold Reed of HRJR Enterprises." Everyone who called me and heard that message was taken by surprise. I would get questions like, "What's that about?" I also got inquiries from some of the bubble busters that I know: "What kind of business do you know how to have?" Like I've said before, the bubble busters are to be ignored while those genuinely interested were enlightened to my vision.

In early 2007, I designed my business cards and began handing them out whenever a networking opportunity presented itself. I had the exact vision as to how I wanted them to come out, and I put it on paper. I went to the printer with a picture and the lettering, and he brought it to life! People were shocked and impressed by my business card as well.

You see, when it comes to sharing what your vision is with people, they are more likely to believe it when they see it rather than see it because you believe it. This being the case, more often than not, it will be vitally necessary that you see your vision, believe in your vision, and strive toward becoming it or bringing it to reality, because if you don't, no one else will.

## Lesson Seven: When Enough is Enough

*The greatest of all mistakes is to do nothing because you think you can only do a little. —Zig Ziglar*

One day a man was taking a walk down an old country road and stopped by his neighbor's house to get a glass of water. When he stepped on his neighbor's porch, he took notice that his neighbor's old hound dog was moaning and groaning. When the neighbor came out, the man asked him, "Why is your dog moaning and groaning?" The neighbor replied, "Oh, he's just sitting on a nail." The man then asked, "Well, then why doesn't he get up?" And the neighbor replied, "Oh, I guess it don't hurt enough."

### What Will It Take For You To Get Up & Take Action?

Everyone reaches a point where they just have to. At first it's instinctual. Look at a baby. One day she's just laying there, and the next she's sitting up. Not too long after that, she's crawling around and then leaning up against things and walking alongside them. Soon after that, she's walking unassisted—and after busting her head and scraping her knees a few times, she's running all around. One day that baby is making gurgling noises. Not too long after that, she's saying, "Mama and Dada," and not too much longer after that, the only time that child is quiet is when she's sleeping! My point, these things tend to occur naturally.

However, as we get older, growth becomes less instinctive. We learn we have the option to act or to not act, and when that happens, we place locks upon our potential, and in order to unlock that potential, there has to be some kind of triggering mechanism. Just for the sake of making this point clearer, I'll broach upon the negative. It is said that in order for an addict to learn he or she has a problem and seek help, they have to hit rock bottom. It is unfortunate that in order to battle one's demons he or she has to face them, but that is a reality of life. But let's get out of the dark and look upon the not so negative. What is it you would like to do? What is it you have always wanted to do but either allowed someone to talk you out of or you talk yourself out of?

In the summer of 2006, I bought my first house. My wife had been hounding me for years to make that move, but I was never ready. I pride myself on not tolerating excuses, but being human, I have to admit that I had many of them. However, my triggering mechanism came when I got my tax return. Even though I was making more money than the previous year, the government was going to see to it that it got a greater chunk of it every year that I was renting an apartment. My number one excuse for not getting a house was that I just could not afford it. Then I read a book called "Rich Dad, Poor Dad" by Robert T. Kiyosaki.

One of the lessons I learned from that book was that for as long as I told myself I could not afford to buy a house, I was not going to be able to afford to buy a house. By telling myself I could not do it, I closed my mind from seeking out and if necessary creating options and solutions. However, when I committed myself to that goal, I unlocked a part of my brain that allowed me to seek out and create those options and solutions. Instead of telling myself what I couldn't do, I began asking myself of what was I capable. I then began looking at the resources and finances I had at my disposal. I then began to develop strategies as to how best use those resources and finances.

The more I pressed forward toward achieving the goal of buying my home, the more resources became available to me. It was then that I learned that when you are focused and committed to achieving your goals, God will provide you with everything you need. You might not get those things when you want them, but you will have them when you need them. Like the old saying goes, "He may not come when you call him, but he's always right on time!" So, I implore you to do what I learned to do. Instead of telling yourself what you "can't" do, ask yourself, "How can I do it?" In one of the lessons in section three, I will go into greater detail about the use of the word can't and how poisonous it is to you experiencing any significant growth or change in your life for the better. Allow me to go back to the example of the developing baby.

Life itself is not very much different at all. Some things just have a natural trigger, but even still, you have to start from somewhere. There will be some bumps and bruises along the way, but in the end—if you are true to yourself and your goals—all of the dark clouds will all have been worth it.

*People who fail to achieve their goals usually get stopped by frustration. They allow frustration to keep them from taking the necessary actions that would support them in achieving their desire. You get through this roadblock by plowing through frustration, taking each setback as feedback you can learn from, and pushing ahead. I doubt you'll find many successful people who have not experienced this. All successful people learn that success is buried on the other side of frustration.*
*—Anthony Robbins*

What is your triggering mechanism going to be? What is it going to take before you step up and step out and tell the universe what you are going to do, have, and/or be? Will it be that bill collector calling you when you're trying to sit down and have dinner, or will it be that next time the bill collector calls, and you get fed up with acting like someone else telling the person that you are not home? Will it be that next time when your idiot of a boss dumps his or her work on you so they can go home early and calls it "delegating responsibility?" Will it be the next time your mate cannot account for his or her whereabouts when they said they were going to be someplace, and they were not there?

Will it be that time you get caught being someplace you yourself were not supposed to be—doing something you had no business doing? Will it actually have to take you facing some demons, or do you think you are capable of just seeing an unacceptable situation as such and just say to yourself, "I'm sick and tired of being sick and tired"? Whatever your triggering mechanism may be, you are going to have to realize within yourself that the time to take action is now. The funny thing is my "now" and your "now" can very well be different times from one another—and even more different from the next person's "now," and that's okay.

However, that being the case, your "now" is up to you, and you have to be the one who determines when it is time for you to fight or flee.

## _Lesson Eight: Have Faith in Yourself First!_

_**Always dream and shoot higher than you know you can reach. Don't bother just to be better than your contemporaries and predecessors; try to be better than yourself. —Unknown**_

Think about everything you've ever done in your life. Now think about how many times you've done a particular thing—the first time you walked and spoke (which you probably can't remember, but you know it happened), the first time you caught a ball, or the first time you ever sank a jump shot. What about the first time you ever drove a car, your first real kiss, or the first time you made love? Anyway ... what do all of these things have in common?

For each and every one of these things, you had to step outside of your comfort zone and cross a line you never crossed before. Also, no matter how much faith your parents, teachers, and friends had in your potential, none of it was relevant until you found the wherewithal within yourself to take action. The easiest way to do something a million and one times is for you to do it just once. Basketball greats Larry Bird and Michael Jordan have both admitted they missed more shots than they made during their careers, yet they remain two of the greatest players to ever play the game.

Tiger Woods, Venus and Serena Williams, all superstars in their given fields, and all of them had great support systems in their families, but where do you think any of them would be if they had not actually decided to take that first step? Tiger Wood's father, Earl Woods, may have put a club in his son's hand and paraded him on national television at the age of four, but that did not guarantee the success Tiger now enjoys. Although he could have just been a great college golfer and got his degree and a nice comfortable job somewhere, Tiger himself made the decision to join the professional ranks. He made that decision because he above all others had faith in his ability to excel.

Venus and Serena Williams have played and won championships on the greatest tennis courts ever constructed in the world, but what would have happened if they did not believe in anything beyond the court their father constructed in their backyard in Compton, California? How many great athletes are there out in the world who could have very well become professional superstars but didn't and don't not because someone has told them or is telling them that they can't succeed but because they are telling themselves that they can't? The answer is probably thousands or even millions worldwide!

Does the name William Hung sound familiar? William Hung was a contestant for the third season of American Idol, a nationally televised talent search. As I have said before, as far as I am concerned, the best part of this show is the first few shows when they are showing the tryouts. They will glaze over the few who will move on to the actual competition, but they spend more time attracting viewers by showing the people who are clearly not suited for such a talent competition. William Hung walked into that hotel ballroom and on national television totally destroyed Ricky Martin's song "She Bangs." If you saw it on television, you know that you're chuckling inside right now just remembering it.

However, the funny thing is that even though he never made it past that horrendous audition, he became more famous than the contestants who were actually chosen to advance in the competition. Between endorsements, a record deal, and a movie deal, William Hung became a millionaire and amassed worldwide fame. Never mind "fifteen minutes of fame," William Hung was on the forefront of international pop culture for about a year, and all because he had enough faith in himself to audition for a nationally televised talent search ... talent be damned! You see, what William suffered and succeeded from was an affliction called "intelligent ignorance." He didn't know that he could not succeed at singing a Ricky Martin song, and as a result he succeeded at singing a Ricky Martin song in spite of what he did not know.

He took a stand before the universe and screamed "She Bangs" with such honesty that after laughing until it hurt, the universe said, "Yeah, we're going to let this one through. He's got it!"

Let's take a look at a person standing out on the ledge of a building, and as sick as it may be, there are dozens of people down on the sidewalk yelling, "Jump! Jump!" and the person may then leap to his death. Are those dozens of idiots to blame? Surely they did not help the situation in a constructive manner, but the fact of the matter is out of all the dozens of voices, the only one that counted was the one that said, "Open the window and climb out onto the ledge." Out of those dozens of voices, the only one that counted was the one that activated the jumper's legs to take that final leap, and that voice was located inside his head.

*You can either rise to great heights or sink to the deepest depths ... if you believe in yourself enough to do so. —HSRjr*

Earlier I said that if people cannot see a larger vision for themselves, it is impossible for them to see a larger vision for you. Here, the opposite applies. You could be the greatest singer to ever grace your shower or church choir but also have the potential to sell out stadiums and sell millions of records; however, if you cannot see it for yourself, what everyone else sees does not count for squat. You must be your own catalyst. Nothing in your life takes form until you take action. Despite all of the encouragement that I received from my friends and fellow Toastmasters, even from my wife, I didn't write this book until I decided within myself that I could. I did not get up and deliver my first speech until I decided that I could.

Everything that you will do in your life will be because you made the decision within yourself to take action. It could be that time you jumped off the highest diving board at the pool or asked the prettiest girl in school to the dance. You didn't have to look like Greg Louganis coming off that diving board. As long as you didn't break your neck going into the water, you proved that you got off that board as many times as you wanted, and with each subsequent dive, you improve your form.

Hey, the prettiest girl might have said no to your offer to dance. At least you had the courage to ask her. And if she said no, then it's her loss! If she couldn't accept you for whatever reason, maybe she wasn't as pretty on the inside as she appeared to be on the outside, and perhaps her saying no was the universe speaking through her because the universe has someone else out there for you.

But since you proved that you could ask that girl, what's stopping you from asking the next girl and next the girl after her? In 1996, I had a job as a Program Director at a karate school called Master Glazier Karate. Basically, it was my job to explain the programs the school offered and then convince people to pay for them. Robert Wetmore, the sensei (head instructor) who I worked directly under, was previously a Program Director who got promoted to running his own school within the chain and trained me to run his school the same way he ran the school for the sensei he had been previously working for.

He showed me how to conduct the introduction meeting, told me exactly what to say, and even how to say it. We would role play, and he would throw every negative response in the book at me—which was not that big of a problem because he even had responses for them! Just like a father holding onto the back of a child riding a bike without training wheels, for the first couple of meetings, he sat in with me just as a safety net. He taught me well because after the first two or three successful enrollments he let me go solo. Then into the school came a woman, who we'll call Carmen, and her two sons. She was a trip. She complained about everything under the sun, and about three or four months later when the time came to sign up her sons for the second portion of their training, I was clearly shaken up.

I was really afraid to have to sit in the office with this woman, and I begged Sensei Wetmore to conduct the meeting. Sensei Wetmore said, "No, you're the Program Director, and you're going to conduct the meeting. You're going to explain to her that if she wants her boys to continue their training then she's going to have to sign them up for it, and she's not going to get any more of a discount than what's listed in the contract. She's either going to say yes or no, but I'll keep my eye on you. And if you think she's going to get out of hand, then give me a signal, but until that happens, she's all yours!"

There were two realities simultaneously at play here. One, he was right. I was the program director and dealing with her was my job, and two, he really didn't want to deal with her any more than I did (and being "the sensei," he really didn't have to)! So, when the day came, I prepared the paperwork and called her into my office when she brought her boys in for class.

Before I could even finish my whole pitch, she just cut me off and said, "My boys love it here; how much is it gonna cost me?" and she handed me her Visa Gold card. She paid for their continuation program in full. We had the papers signed and completed in less than five minutes. Sensei Wetmore, who was teaching a class, watched as Carmen walked out of my office and was just about to come off the mat to "save" me. When I saw him approaching, I walked over to the window separating my office from the dojo (classroom) and held up a sign that had only three letters on it: "P.I.F." which stood for "Paid In Full."

From that point on, he never had to come in and save me. When I first got out of the police academy, I rode with senior officers whose assignment was to train me and my fellow "rookies." Whomever I rode with, I followed his lead. I did not speak if he did not speak. I did not advance unless he advanced, and I did not go for my weapon until he went for his, unless I perceived a threat he could not see. When two officers ride together, one assumes the role of the "contact officer," who is the one that does the talking. The other officer assumes the role of the "cover officer."

His or her role is to just observe the scene and be on the lookout for any potential threats. For about three weeks, I rode with an officer named Kearse, and I followed my same pattern with him—he was the contact officer, and I was the cover officer. One night, we were dispatched to a domestic disturbance, a husband and wife argument.

When we got there, I took up a position in the apartment where I could see my partner and where he could see me, and we both commenced to listening to both sides of the altercation. When both the husband

and wife stated their cases, I looked at Kearse to see what he was going to say and how he was going to solve their problem. Kearse in turn looked at me, pointed both his index fingers at me, and said, "You're on!" under his breath. Bam … now all eyes in the apartment were on me. It's a good thing I was paying attention on those previous jobs because I handled the situation with ease. From that night on, whenever Kearse and I rode together, he would fall back and have me be the contact officer.

While some of my other classmates rode with a senior officer that was more concerned with having his or her "senior" status respected, I was partnered with a cop who wanted to train me to do the job so that when my day came to be the senior officer in the car assigned to train a new cop, I would be able to do just that, train him/her and not control him/her. Riding with Kearse increased both my knowledge and my confidence.

Within three months, out of all of my academy classmates, I was the first one assigned to ride solo, and I was also assigned one of the busiest patrol sectors in the city. Whatever was going to happen in the city of East Orange was going to happen in my patrol sector, and when it did, if I was assigned to the job, I held it down.

It's good if you already have a support system showing you they have faith in your abilities, but if you never build up the courage to take action, then you stand a very strong chance of losing that support system. You don't even necessarily have to be fearless, but all you need is just enough courage to take that first step and the next. Before you know it, you have created a courageous snowball effect, and you are on your way!

### _Lesson Nine: What is Your Greatest Challenge?_

**_When you've got something to prove there's nothing greater than a challenge. —Terry Bradshaw_**

If you are truly on your path to self-improvement, then you have to come to some kind of realization that certain changes need to be made in your life. So, let's talk about what you want to change. You see, it's one thing to say, "I need to make some changes in my life," and it's another thing to say, "I need to change 'this'—I need to change 'that.'" In order to make some kind of positive change, you need to deal in specifics. You can't be like Captain Kirk and just say, "Make a left at the second star and go on till morning."

You need to know what in life it is that you want to change. You need to have a destination. Do you want to lose weight? Gain muscle? Become more attractive to the opposite sex? Gain more confidence so that you can go after the man or woman of your dreams? Or do you want to get a better paying job, or even better, start your own business? Before you take any kind of action toward doing something, logic tells us that we must first know what it is we want to do.

**_God does not change the condition of people until they change within themselves._**
**_—The Holy Qur'an—Surat ar-Ra'ad: 13:11_**

**_The Phases of Goal Setting_**

**_1. Write it down._** This is the very start of the goal-setting phase. When you write your goals down, they take form. They become tangible as opposed to ideas that can fade away with life's other distractions. I had an instructor once tell me (regarding writing detailed police reports), "If it's not down there in black and white, it never happened." Put your goals on paper and then put them somewhere you can see them every day, so you know what it is you've set out to do.

**2. You must know why you are taking a particular action.** Why do you want to achieve a particular goal? What do you expect to gain by achieving your goal? What are your motivating factors? If you are truly on your path to self-improvement, you should not be intentionally taking actions that will lead toward losing outcomes. Remember, we are talking about self-improvement, improving ourselves from within. So, it is extremely vital that you know why you are putting forth your effort. Why should you know why? Keep on reading!

*If you know why you can overcome any how.*
*—Les Brown*

**3. How are you going to achieve your goals?** Before explaining this, I must reiterate that if you do not know what you want to do, why becomes irrelevant—as does how you will do it because without knowing what you want to do, you'll never get to how. So, when you have an idea of what you want to do (an idea is all you have), you need to dig deeper into yourself and find out why you're going to do it. After that comes the difficult, yet most exciting, part, and that is trying to figure out how you're going to do it.

This is where you plan your work and determine which will be your best courses of action. Now, the key thing to remember here is that you are the boss. You get to make the decisions of what you will do and what you won't do. Can you get away with taking a little shortcut, or should you go the long way? There are different ways to do different things. Which ways will you choose?

**4. Do it, review it, then redo it.** Remember, "The journey of a thousand miles begins with the first step." Just as what you want to do is irrelevant if you do not know why you're going to do it, what, why, and how are all irrelevant if you do nothing—and even more so if what you are doing is not working. You must take action in order to achieve results. None of us are perfect, and as my father often says, "The best laid plans of mice and men often go awry."

So just because you have devised a strategy to achieve your goal, that alone does not mean it will totally work. You may have to tweak your strategy here and there; lest we not forget, Mr. Murphy's Law is either on his way to your home or is already camped out in your backyard! Make sure that what you're doing is working. If it's not, make the necessary changes and then jump back into the fray!

Think about your favorite sport. In football and basketball, if the first few plays don't appear to be working, the team calls a time-out, after which the team goes back out with a new game plan. Even in boxing, the fighters' corner men are giving them new and different strategies in between rounds—even during the rounds!

***Do not pray for an easy life, pray for the strength to endure a difficult one. —Bruce Lee***

What about when you get in your car to go someplace? You don't just pull out of your driveway, go in a straight line, and end up at your destination (unless you're going to visit the person across the street!). No, you go to the corner, make a turn, and then go another distance and make another turn, and repeat this process until you arrive at your destination. As long as you know your destination, you can deal with the twists and turns along the way.

Overcoming your greatest challenges, or even your smaller ones, may not be easy. Remember, nothing worth having comes easy. However, the chances are the harder the challenge, the harder the struggle, and thus, the sweeter the victory! Take the story of former heavyweight champion James "Buster" Douglas, the fighter who broke Mike Tyson's undefeated winning streak (and also the image of Tyson's invincibility). Mike Tyson was being hailed pound for pound as the greatest boxer on the planet, and just when it seemed he was unstoppable, this janitor who few ever heard of, who pretty much had nothing to lose, surprised the entire world by handing Mike Tyson his first knockout!

Here was a man who was pretty much considered to be yet another victim to one of Tyson's first-round knockouts; however, the man who came to fight was a man on a mission. His mother had recently passed away, and only a handful of people believed in his chances to win, yet this man stepped into the ring and did the impossible.

***The impossible is only impossible because you haven't stepped up to make it possible. —HSRjr***

Ask yourself—what is standing in your way? Grab a pen and piece of paper and make up a list of your obstacles. Don't grab a pencil! Pencils come with erasers. Grab a pen (with non-erasable ink) and commit to what it is you're writing down. Sit there for as long as it takes. You can never be convicted of wasting time if the time is spent thinking or even dreaming of ways you can go about improving your life. So, what's holding you back or standing in your way? Bubble busters? A jerk of a boss? Lack of money? Lack of spare time? Get yourself about a good five to ten items on that list.

Once you've compiled that list, categorize those items in terms of what's holding you back the most down to what's holding you back the least. At the top of that list, you will find your greatest challenge. Your mission— should you choose to accept it: brainstorm and create ways to tackle, defeat, and overcome that challenge. Once you've conquered your greatest challenge, the rest should be progressively easier to knock out. Rudolph Giuliani, who was knighted "America's Mayor" after the horrific terrorist attack on September 11, 2001, once stated, "When you confront a problem you begin to solve it."

## Our Greatest Fear

*Our greatest fear is not that we are inadequate, but that we are powerful beyond measure. It is our light, not our darkness that frightens us.*

*We ask ourselves, who am I to be brilliant, gorgeous, handsome, talented and fabulous? Actually, who are you not to be? You are a child of God. Your playing small does not serve the world. There is nothing enlightened about shrinking so that other people won't feel insecure around you.*

*We were born to make manifest the glory of God within us. It is not just in some; it is in everyone. And, as we let our own light shine, we consciously give other people permission to do the same.*

*As we are liberated from our fear, our presence automatically liberates others.*

*Marianne Williamson*

## Lesson Ten: Leadership

*If your actions inspire others to dream more, learn more, do more and become more, you are a leader.*
*—John Quincy Adams*

As I explained in a previous lesson, when you go about finding your way, you have to create momentum in order to see results. As your momentum increases, the universe will put the necessary people and resources into your life to help you along the way. However, success does not come free. First of all, you will have to prove yourself worthy of being successful. Once you've done that, you will find you have an obligation to give something back. There are many different ways in which this can be accomplished. This particular lesson will reflect upon one that is close to my heart. One of the main ways you can give back for what you've gained is to teach or mentor someone coming up behind you.

There's an old Chinese proverb that says, "When the student is ready, the teacher will present himself." Leadership is one of the many responsibilities one must shoulder in order to maintain success. Every successful person has a powerful team backing him or her up. However, the mark of a truly good leader is one who can build people up to become successful in their own right and shine in their own light. There have been a few times in my life where I have been placed in positions of leadership. For me, I believe it was the universe's way of making me grow up. However, where I am in my life now, I find myself using the lessons I learned to try to help people see the greatness that exists within them.

My first true taste of leadership was thrust upon me at the tender age of nineteen. I was in basic training, and the drill instructor made it so just by saying it. For the following six weeks, anyone wearing a "Smokey the

Bear" style hat on his or her head was as close to God on earth as I was going to get. The drill instructor who made that appointment was a man named Sgt. Franklin Skidmore. Now, I cannot use his exact words, but let's just say that he let me know in no uncertain terms that I would have to answer to him for any and all mistakes or acts of stupidity regardless of if they were my fault or that of any of my fellow recruits. It was not like I had much of a choice.

As a matter of fact, even before I knew of the actual phrase, I knew in my mind and in my heart that failure was not an option. Without warning, I was thrust into a position where I had to lead a group of men, most of whom were older than me, and I knew just as much, if not less, about being in the military as they did. We did well as a team over the course of those six weeks.

There were ups and downs, but there were more ups than there were downs, and ultimately I believe the reason for our success was the fact that I relied on them to do what we were all trained to do, which was follow orders and work hard at getting things done right the first time—and do it together. Ever since that point in my life, I have had other experiences in leadership positions where I fared well and others not so well, and I have learned from both my successes as well as my setbacks.

What I have learned is that leadership is more than being in a position where you get to tell people what to do. Leadership is about building and guiding. It is about creating opportunities to succeed using the talents of those under your leadership. People often think leaders are born. Leaders are not born. Leaders are made. Leaders are created. Leaders are nothing if they are not first followers themselves.

*The best executive is the one who has sense enough to pick good men to do what he wants, and self-restraint to keep from meddling with them while they do it. —Theodore Roosevelt*

People who are justly put in positions of leadership are put there because they have experience that can be used to benefit the collective. Notice, I said "justly." There are often times when you will encounter people who are in positions of leadership based more on who they know rather than what they know.

Don't get me wrong, it's good to network and utilize connections to attain certain positions or get certain things accomplished, but it is better to be able to have the knowledge or skills required to achieve higher levels of success. It's one thing to know someone who knows someone who can get you into a high-paying job, but what happens when you get into that job and you do not have the skills to actually do that job? You wind up making a fool out of both yourself and the person who "hooked you up."

However, there are those in such positions who do well because they know how to effectively utilize the talents of those under them. Ultimately, that's a great skill to possess; however, should the leader solely take credit for what the team has done, well, that's just wrong. A truly good leader is one who can utilize his or her team's talents to achieve an objective then allow the entire team to share in the accolades should the end result be successful. Unfortunately, should the end result not be successful, the leader has to be the one who accepts responsibility for the team's failure. My father used to always tell me, "You've got to pay the cost to be the boss." I found out in my early thirties that he got that saying from an old James Brown song, but it's very much true, nonetheless.

***Uneasy lies the head that wears a crown.***
***—William Shakespeare***

The reality is no one likes being told what to do. How many of you like being told what to do? Before I left basic training, my head drill instructor, Staff Sgt. Robert Yee, told me that he called ahead to my next duty station and recommended me for a student leadership position. He also told me that people often took those positions in order to be able to try to get some payback against their dorm chiefs from basic training, but dorm chiefs were automatically considered for those leadership positions above all others.

Any of you who were ever in the military and who carried the burdens I carried over that period of time know that when it was over, all you wanted was just to be another face in the crowd. Staff Sgt. Yee knew this about me, and he knew I was not going to volunteer for one of those positions, but he saw something in me that I had yet to see in myself. When I arrived at my next duty station, my name was already known amongst the cadre of command in my squadron. They told me that Staff Sgt. Yee had in fact called them. He told them that they should make me a student leader without giving me a choice, just as they had done in basic training.

Fortunately, they could not make me a student leader if I did not want to be one. On the flip side, even though no one that was under my command in basic training was in my new squadron, when word got out that I was a dorm chief, I became a target to total strangers—just the kind of vindictive people that Staff Sgt. Yee warned me about. The end result ... I could not stand being in a position where I was being ordered around by people who were just plain unfit to do so, so I wound up becoming a student leader anyway.

This leads me to another important aspect of leadership, that being: once you've done it and done it well, it's virtually impossible to be able to tolerate being led by someone you believe to be unworthy or incompetent. However, one of the best characteristics of a good leader is one who knows when to fall back and follow for the greater good. Ultimately, everyone is answerable and held accountable to someone. A good leader knows this and is humbled by this. Sometimes you have to step up and take the crown.

For various reasons which I cannot get into, I was inspired to run for the office of national president of my fraternal organization Groove Phi Groove Social Fellowship Incorporated®. Ultimately, I felt that there were certain changes that needed to be made, and when I made the decision to run for the position, I felt that I was the best man for the job. I didn't win that election, but hindsight being 20/20, I came to the realization that God uses us as he sees fit—many times without us even being aware of it. He also rewards us for our faithful service.

When I made the decision to run for that office, it was because no one else had stepped up to do so, and it didn't look like anyone was going to. When I made it known that I was "going for the crown" so to speak, it woke up the brother who ran against me, who should have thrown his hat in the ring long before it was even an idea in my head. I was his catalyst and a worthy opponent. His victory was a close one and in the end what was best for the organization at the time. I may not have returned home a national president; however, what I did gain was all of the time I would have had to sacrifice away from my family in fulfilling my presidential duties.

*The quality of a leader is reflected in the standards they set for themselves. —Ray Kroc*

Everyone is not suited to lead; however, leaders are not born—they are made. They are either forged by the fire of having to take immediate action, are groomed over time, or self-made. In my life, I have experienced all of these areas. In boot camp, I was thrown into the position. With regards to my aspiration to lead my fellowship, the decision was not a spur of the moment thing. Hindsight being 20/20, I can honestly say that this decision was fifteen years in the making.

In deciding to become a speaker and an author, I would have to say that the process was more like ten years in the making. I began reading a few books in the late nineties that really helped me turn my life around and learn how to start digging my feet in the ground while facing the universe and demanding my place in it. In 2006, when I began reevaluating my life and determining what new goals I needed to set for myself, I decided that I wanted to assume another more subtle role of leadership. By that, I mean I will share with your ideas and experiences that have worked for me. If you follow them, then you follow me. Whatever it is you want to do in life, do it well.

However, once you've learned to do it well, share it with others. Pass it on. This is how legacies are created. This is how many family-owned businesses have been able to stay in existence for decades and some even over a century. Leadership is not about being the boss over people. Understanding and exercising good leadership is what is necessary in order for you to find a way to make a way!

*My goal is to take the quality of my life as high as I can so that when my time comes "to go," hopefully I won't have to go too far to reach my final destination. —HSRjr*

# SECTION THREE: GO!

## Lesson One: I Can't Say "I Can't"

*Ability is what you're capable of doing. Motivation determines what you do. Attitude determines how well you do it. —Lou Holtz*

Let us revisit an example we've used already. Remember that misplaced hairbrush, comb, wallet, or keys to your car that we talked about before? Or wait—the remote control to your television set? Did you drive everyone else in the house crazy running around trying to find that thing telling them, "I can't find it" only to have a house member come along and pick it up right off of the dresser or coffee table and say, "Here it is right under your nose"? The reason why they were able to find it and you were not is all about the difference in motivation and mindset between the two of you.

You were running around saying, "I can't," while the other person came into the room with the goal to find the misplaced item so they could be spared from you driving them crazy tearing the place apart. In a previous lesson, I stated the two most powerful words in the English language are "I am." Consequently, the two of the most devastating words to ever be put together in the English language are I and can't. When those two words are put together, your fate is pretty much sealed. When you say, "I can't," you instantly shut your mind to any future possibilities.

For about a good three years, my wife would occasionally harass me about buying a house, and I would always tell her that was something I couldn't afford to do. The more I told her—and myself—that I could not afford to buy a house, the more I was able to successfully fulfill that particular prophecy. My outlook changed when I read the book Rich Dad, Poor Dad by Robert T. Kiyosaki. In the book he tells how his friend's father, his "rich dad," taught him how to view money and wealth differently from the way his real father, his "poor dad," viewed them. One of the lessons he learned was that the poor and middle class tend to focus on what they "can't" afford, whereas the rich instead ask of themselves the question, "How can I afford it?"

With that, I began asking that question of myself, and about three to four months later, my family moved out of our two-bedroom apartment and into our four-bedroom home. When you make a statement, the buck tends to stop right there. When you ask questions, you leave the door open for possibilities. As a matter of fact, let's look deeper into what I just said. When you make a statement, it's like closing a door. I guess a good or bad outcome would depend on which side of the door you happen to be on.

Asking a question is like leaving the door open, and when the door is left open, anything can happen. When you say, "I can't," you eliminate the potential for a possibility to rise, and you instantly hamper what you are capable of. When you ask, "How can I?" you leave your mind open to explore all kinds of possibilities. Consequently, when you say, "I can," you are affirming what you are capable of. In short, if you say, "I can't," then you won't, and there will be absolutely no one you have to blame for your lack of capability … but yourself.

That one phrase alone has made both kings and queens, and also bums, out of many men and women since the beginning of time. Everything you have in your home that you couldn't imagine living life without was invented by someone who at some point said, "I can't say I can't."

Look at the most successful people you admire, and you will be looking at people who did not succumb to the evil power of the words I can't. There was a time when a woman was told she couldn't sit in a particular section of a bus. She ignored that person, and when Rosa Parks sat down, a nation of people stood up and changed the world. Where would Oprah Winfrey be if she believed that she could not overcome her many obstacles? Where would Michael Jordan be if, after missing a shot for the first time, he believed he couldn't become the greatest to ever play the game of basketball?

*Most people have no idea of the giant capacity we can immediately command when we focus all of our resources on mastering a single area of our lives.*
*—Anthony Robbins*

You will never be able to find a way to make a way if you succumb to the evil power of the words I can't. Remember, the universe exists to give you what you want in life, and the only price it demands is that you prove yourself worthy. However, when you say, "I can't," you are slamming the door in the face of both God and the universe. When you ask, "How can I?" you begin to open that door to all kinds of possibilities. Some of them could be absolutely ridiculous—and also wind up being the ones that make you a fortune!

In the sixties, an inventor and chemist by the name of Spencer F. Silver was trying to make a super-adhesive. Instead, he created a substance that was a high-quality but "low-tack" adhesive, made of very small, virtually indestructible acrylic spheres that would stick only where they were tangent to a given surface rather than flat up against it. What resulted was that the adhesive's grip was strong enough to hold papers together but weak enough to allow the papers to be pulled apart again without being torn. Even more importantly, the adhesive could be used in the same way again and again. Now, Silver, who was a senior chemist for the 3M Company, wanted to market the adhesive as a spray or as a surface for bulletin boards on which temporary notices could be easily posted and then removed.

For five years, he held marketing seminars trying to get both his colleagues and the higher-ups to buy into his latest creation, but none of them would hear of it. For whatever reasons, they were all saying that this product "can't" sell. That is until another man, Arthur Fry, attended one of Silver's seminars about the product. In his spare time, Fry would sing in his church choir. Unfortunately, whenever he would stand up to sing, the bookmark he was using to hold his place in the hymn book would fall out.

However, during a particularly boring sermon, his mind wandered back to Silver's seminar and how his not-so-super adhesive could be used as a bookmark that would not fall out. When Fry returned to work, he drew up a proposal and handed out hundreds of samples of the product to people in his office.

Originally, the 3M executives were back on board that "can't" train again, but after they saw how much of a buzz was being created by the samples that Fry was handing out, they gave the product its full support. After about another five years of perfecting the product's specifications and developing the machines necessary to mass-produce the product, Post-its were born!

For years, many highly educated and well-renowned doctors said it was not only physically impossible but practically fatal for a person to be able to run a four minute mile. Then on May 6, 1954, a man by the name of Roger Bannister made fools out of all of them by being the first man ever to run a mile in under four minutes. Bannister ran a mile in three minutes and 59.4 seconds. The four-minute mile has been run countless times by thousands of runners both amateur and professional all over the world ever since.

I have said it once or twice before, and I will say it again. The only thing you need in order to be able to do something a million and one times is to do it just once. In a great many cases in life, just like with Bannister's four minute mile, all you need is to see that someone else has done it. In case you haven't noticed, I have very deep feelings with regards to my fraternal organization. Those feelings are such because I learned a great deal during my pledge process, and I continue to learn many valuable life lessons as a full member. When I meet new candidates seeking membership into my fellowship, one of the things I tell them is, "The only difference between you and me is that I got here first.

I am no better a man than you, and you are no better a man than me. If I could do it, there is no reason why you can't … unless you believe within yourself that you can't." I submit to you that if you take that same mindset when you look up to any person you deem successful and study and emulate what they have done, you could very well find yourself celebrating some level of success of your own.

## Lesson Two: Become an "Active" Thinker Immediately

*Watch your thoughts, for they become words. Watch your words, for they become actions. Watch your actions, for they become habits. Watch your habits, for they become character. Watch your character, for it becomes your destiny. —Unknown*

What do you say when a person asks, "How are you doing?" Do you respond as to how you are really feeling, or do you give a preprogrammed response? Have you ever observed people exchange pleasantries like, "Hey, how are you?" "Fine and you?" but the people actually keep going in different directions without that last question being answered? How are you feeling? Do you even know? I read a book called "Better Than Good" by Zig Ziglar, one of the greatest if not the greatest motivational speaker in the world. In the beginning of the book, he states that when people ask him how he's doing, he replies, "I'm doing better than good," and then he makes mention of how people are somewhat taken aback by that particular response because it is not a preprogrammed response to such a general question—a question that is more of a courtesy than it is an actual inquiry about one's genuine concern for another.

In the book, he invites you to take the "better than good" response and incorporate it into your daily life, which is what I have done. When someone asks me, "Hey, how ya doin'?" I reply, "I'm doing better than good, better than most." I too have experienced somewhat of a pause from people simply because they were not expecting that particular reply, but what shocked me the most would be what they would say back to me after that. They would say, "Well, that's good." I found that to be extremely interesting. Didn't I just say I was doing "better than good"? This leads me to two conclusions. The first of which being people do not listen. They react not to what you told them yourself but what they tell themselves you said. The second conclusion is the realization that most people go through life with blinders on. They accept things as they happen without much, if any, questioning. If something good happens, great! If something bad happens, however, after a whole lot of complaining ... nothing.

*There are three kinds of people: (1) Those who make things happen; (2) Those who watch things happen; and (3) Those who don't know what happened. —Unknown*

When you make a conscious effort to take stock of your attitude and your thinking, you automatically give yourself a "one-up" on the average person. How? The average person does not actively think. For the average person, he or she exerts about as much effort into thinking as he or she does into breathing, and since breathing is an involuntary function of the body, each thought is more or less like a breath ... in, out, then gone. An "active" thinker asks questions. Look at your typical five- to ten-year-old child. He asks a million and two questions all beginning with the same word: why? However, at some point in the growing process, this questioning of things either slows down or stops entirely. When this happens, it is truly a sad thing because at that point the person stops "growing" and starts "aging." The difference between the two is similar to the difference between thinking and breathing:

Thinking/Growing: A conscious act.

Breathing/Aging: Requires no effort at all.

I love movies. I like to correlate a lot of my life's lessons to some of the things I have seen in movies, sort of like a "life imitates art" kind of thing. Take the Star Wars series of movies for example. In these movies, there are characters called "Jedi." Now, I'm not going to get all "Sci-Fi" on you, but if you haven't seen at least one Star Wars movie in the past twenty years or so, I can only ask, "What planet have you been on?" Anyway, the Jedi have extraordinary abilities, but the one most relevant here is their power of mental persuasion. With a mere waving of the hand and a soft spoken word, a Jedi can completely change a person's thinking.

Excluding the whole "mystical" aspect, this act is not too far off from what can actually be accomplished in an exchange between an "active" thinker and an average person. Con artists do it all the time. Basically, if you are convincing enough, you actually can change a person's thinking. Advertising companies make millions on top of millions of dollars a year by making things so appealing that you just have to jump right off of your couch and spend your money.

Advertising executives are "active" thinkers in their particular field, and thus they are often the shepherds amongst the flock of sheep otherwise known as average-thinking consumers. So how do you become an "active" thinker? Well, simply put—like the old Nike slogan says, "Just Do It." But just in case you need a little kick start, try these two techniques:

1. Find that five- to ten-year-old child inside of you and start asking why again.

2. Do not wait for someone to give you the answers— seek them out for yourself!

After all, if someone else gives you all the answers, you aren't "actively" thinking, are you?

***There are two kinds of people: some willing to work, and the rest willing to let them. —Robert Frost***

I have come to learn this to be true in so many different areas of my life. There have been times when I became what I choose to call a "victim of my own success." What this means is that I would perform a particular task or function so well that I would not be allowed to move on to something else. This is a bittersweet situation to be in, but it's better to be considered an asset than it is to be considered a liability.

When they operate for the greater good, "active" thinkers are assets. So … I now challenge you to find your inner "Jedi." I challenge you to take off your blinders and start looking around and asking questions. I challenge you to stop just letting things happen around you and to you and start "actively" thinking about how you can make things happen around you and for you.

*As you begin changing your thinking, start immediately to change your behavior. Begin to act the part of the person you would like to become. Take action on your behavior. Too many people want to feel, then take action. This never works. — John Maxwell*

The most successful people in the world are "active" thinkers. Russell Simmons dropped out of City College in New York in the mid-late seventies to promote parties and small-time club concerts. He took a small and relatively unknown genre of music called rap and an even lesser known inner-city culture known as hip-hop and in 1984 changed the face of music all over the world by starting Def Jam Records, a business he created in his dorm room and sold some fifteen years later for one hundred million dollars—that's one hundred million dollars!

Another internationally known and respected mogul, founder of Bad Boy Records, Sean "Diddy" Combs, was a college student at Howard University who would commute back to New York on the weekends for an unpaid intern position with a record company. In less than ten years he went from being an unpaid intern to a world-famous music mogul. He even went on to hire the man who once fired him some several years earlier. Debbi Fields and her husband started their business in the late seventies and have become multimillionaires. Oh, you don't know who Debbi Fields is?

The next time you have a craving for some oatmeal raisin chocolate chip cookies, go to your local mall and look up "Mrs. Fields" on the mall directory! "Active" thinkers are some scary people. These are truly the "talented tenth" of the world. They don't allow themselves to be pigeon-holed and boxed in. "Active" thinkers have no time in their lives for bubble busters; as a matter of fact, "active" thinkers laugh at bubble busters. "Active" thinkers do not go through life on autopilot— that is, unless they are sitting in their own private jets! The best salespeople in the world are "active" thinkers.

The best salespeople in the world have more than likely been rejected many more times than they have made successful sales, but as a result, they became better equipped to counter future rejections, thus improving their successful sales.

***Thought is action in rehearsal. —Unknown***

Another way to say this is to plan your work then work your plan. "Active" thinkers don't sit on their duffs; they put plans into motion. After all, the key word here is "active," and the root of that word is "act." Average thinkers focus on problems. "Active" thinkers focus on solving problems. "Active" thinkers acknowledge problems and seek out solutions. Average thinkers see unfortunate circumstances as situations they are prisoners to while "active" thinkers see unfortunate circumstances as obstacles that are meant to be overcome and as prisons from which they must escape.

I am an "active" thinker because I analyze everything! I make a conscious effort to see things not only how I want them to be but how someone else might want them to be. I might get into a friendly debate with a relative, friend, or fellowman, and I know when I've arrived at the point where I'm wearing them down because they will say something like, "You're reading too much into this." Here's some food for thought. When a person says something like that to you, he or she is admitting that they may not be as adept at the given topic of discussion, or at the very least they are not at the level of understanding that you are.

Or ... as I said, you've worn them down. In closing, don't just look at the world around you— see it. Don't just hear what people say to and around you—listen. Take nothing for granted and analyze everything. Some things you will discard; actually, most of the things around you will probably be discarded, but for those things that you do take in, you will get so much more out of them. When you go about making a conscious effort to see things from various points of view, you give yourself different options in terms of how you will proceed.

More often than not, you will come out on top of and far ahead of those average thinkers that are just reacting to whatever happens to them.

## _Lesson Three: Failure Is Not an Option – It's an Opportunity_

_Defeat doesn't finish a man—quitting does. A man is not finished when he's defeated. He's finished when he quits. —Richard M. Nixon_

The word failure is defined as nonperformance of something due, required, or expected. For the record, I do not spend a lot of time dwelling on failure. I've got too many other more important things to focus my energies on; however, at the same time, as the saying goes, it is wise for one to know thy enemy, and if ever there was an enemy to success, failure is it. This lesson is going to be really short. Take it in—then take it out! For the longest time I have used the phrase "Failure is not an option" to motivate myself and others. I have since come to the realization that I have been cheating both myself and those with whom I have used that phrase.

You see, what I have come to learn is that failure is not the end of a situation unless you allow it to be. How many times have you gotten into a car and after driving around for a while realize that you're lost because somewhere on the trip you turned right when you should have turned left or vice versa? At that point when you realized you made a wrong turn, did you just turn back and go home? No, you would pull over and seek out directions and get back on track to arriving at your destination. Life works in a similar fashion.

First, I'm going to tell you why failure is not an option. Another word for failure is "setback," and as you follow your path in life, you encounter setbacks in order to learn what is not going to work. Encountering a setback is like making that wrong turn and finding yourself approaching a dead end street. You simply turn around and seek out your correct course. Failure is not an option because the word option is only another word for choice, and who in their right mind chooses to fail?

Keep in mind that the operative words here are in their right mind. How many people do you know who never really do anything above and beyond what's required because they don't think it will do any good? These are life's failures—remember, failure is not the end of a situation unless you allow it to be, and if you make a conscious decision to go above and beyond, you will fail—to succeed.

Now, I'll tell you why failure is an opportunity. If you know where you want to go and encounter setbacks along the way, with each setback you have an opportunity to overcome them. If you hurt your friend's feelings—either on purpose or by accident—for that particular incident, you failed to be a true friend. Now, if your act was done purposefully, then you chose to fail at being a friend; however, if your act was in fact an accident, you have an opportunity to make amends.

How many things have you failed at? There has to be something. I believe that there is God within us all, but none of us are God, so none of us are perfect; therefore, you have failed at something. Baseball players strike out; they miss pop flies, and they run into walls trying to make the big catch. Basketball players miss free throws, three-pointers, and jump shots from all angles. Football players fumble and quarterbacks throw interceptions, but the game does not end at the first strikeout, missed basket, or fumble.

The game goes on—life goes on. Failure is not an option— it's an opportunity! Whatever you did today—good, bad, or indifferent— it's done! If you did well today, come tomorrow all you have to show for it is a good memory of what you did. If you did not do well today, well then, you failed to do well today—but so what? Tomorrow … tomorrow, if by God's grace you wake up tomorrow, you have an opportunity to evaluate where you went wrong yesterday and make it right today—and if you don't, so what!

Every day is a new chance to get it right. Every day is a chance to get just that much closer to the brass ring. Nothing worth having comes easy; if it did, you wouldn't appreciate it. So, it's okay if you stumble along the way. Again, like my mentor Les Brown says, "When life knocks you down—and it will—try to land on your back, because if you can look up, you can get up!"

Failure is not an option—it's an opportunity!

### _Lesson Four: Use Your Motto_

_**Just as you are the one who has to endure and overcome your own personal trials and obstacles, you have to be the one to find your own motto.**_
_**—HSRjr**_

Ever since 12:19 a.m., December 20, 1992, I have been a proud member of Groove Phi Groove Social Fellowship Incorporated. The period of time I spent during my pledge process to this very day remains to be several of the most significantly developmental weeks of my entire life. Even though just two and a half years prior I was pushing earth (doing push-ups) at the crack of dawn in boot camp at Lackland Air Force Base in San Antonio, Texas (which has some days in early spring that are two degrees shy of Dante's Inferno), that experience—although also significantly developmental—could not compare to my pledge experience.

The reason: choices. I had no choice but to endure the rigors of boot camp. I signed a legally binding contract, and breaking said contract could lead to imprisonment ("Drop and give you twenty-five? Sir, yes, sir!"). When I was pledging, that was a situation I could have walked away from at any point in time, and there were a couple of times where I almost took advantage of that privilege. However, one of my Potential Fellowmen asked me a question that has stuck with me—and that I even use—to this very day: "If you quit this, what else are you going to quit in life when things get hot?"

That question hit me like a bolt of lightning! I had no answer for it. It was a straight but loaded question because there is no answer to it, at least none I could give and keep my dignity. On the first night of my pledge process, I was given a series of words I had to commit to memory. Those words were only to be referred to as "my motto," and whenever I was faced with a task or challenge or an assignment given by a potential fellowman, I had to use "my motto" to find a way to achieve that task, challenge, or assignment.

Now, since I am sworn to secrecy, I cannot share with you what "my motto" is; however, what I can tell you is that group of words inspired me to get things done and make things happen, and I still use "my motto" to this very day! What is a motto? A motto is defined as "a sentence, phrase, or word expressing the spirit or purpose of a person or an organization." Having to endure obstacles of one sort or another is just a reality of life. You cannot avoid it. You wake up late; your car won't start; you miss the bus or train; the weatherman said it was going to be clear skies all day, and just when you get out the door and halfway to your car, it starts raining. And I know this has happened to somebody reading this book.

It's Friday and you've got a hot date planned, but just when you're about to walk out that door, your supervisor lands a big assignment on your desk that you cannot afford to waste a single minute on, and your hot date ends up turning into a cold shower! When these things happen, chances are you're not going to be in a position where you can pull out this book to get motivation (however, if you do have time at that moment to pull out a book for motivation, let it be some kind of prayer book or other form of spiritual scripture).

For a quick motivational fix, you will need a motto of your own. You need to have your own special "sentence, phrase, or word expressing the spirit or purpose" of what it is you need to fight harder and carry on. Having a motto of your own will give you that push you need to see you through. Now, this can't be just a catch phrase or cliché. Your motto has to really mean something to you. It has to hit you like a shot of espresso. You could drink a big cup of coffee, but you're not going to drink any espresso in the same size cup!

Your motto needs to be something easy for you to remember but significant enough to where it packs a big punch. Your motto has to be something that lights a fire under your bottom, opens your mind, and helps you put things into proper perspective, but quickly.

### *Where Can I Get My Motto?*

That's easy! You can find your motto anywhere. It can be an old saying that your grandmother used to always say. You can get it from any number of books you may have read. The best place—if you're asking me—to get yourself a motto is in your Bible, Qur'an, Torah, or any holy scripture you find spiritual peace in. After all, the purpose of your motto is to give you a quick shot of motivation, and where better a place to find that than in a book of Holy Scripture? Again, it doesn't necessarily have to come from Scripture, but that's as best a place as any to start looking for one. You can have a motto for every occasion like I do. Here are some favorites that I can share with you:

When dealing with "less than honest" people:

"An honest man has no need for a long memory—but it doesn't hurt to have one to be able to know when you're not dealing with honest men." (I believe Abraham Lincoln is the creator of the first half, but the second half is mine!)

"If you throw a stone into a pack of dogs, the one that hollers is the one you hit." (In other words, if you walk into a room and say "Somebody in here lied to me," those who did not lie to you aren't worried about what you just said, but the one who comes to you wanting to know more about what you mean could very well be the one who lied to you!)

Greeting:

"Hey, how are you?" {Response}: "Better than good, better than most; too deep in my groove to be moved; too blessed to be stressed, too anointed to be disappointed!"

"Hey, how's it goin'?" {Response}: "Every day above the dirt and below the radar is a good day!"

Retribution:

"God don't like ugly, and Karma is an S.O.B.!"

I could go on for probably another whole five or six pages; as I said, I have mottos for just about every single occasion. However, since I cannot walk your life's journey for you, it would be totally unfair to you and irresponsible of me to spoon-feed you such a list. Just as you are the one who has to endure and overcome your own personal trials and obstacles, you have to be the one to find your own motto. Plus, the way I see it, I'm giving you a great head start. I was given one motto. Here I have just given you five! When you go about searching for your motto, you also enrich your soul. As you read Scripture or even this book (not to equate this book to Scripture on any level), when you find a quote or passage that you find comfort in, if it moves and inspires you, you own it—so store it, use it, and repeat it!

# Lesson Five: First Success Story: The Difference Between Earning Money and Making Money

*Success is the result of making the right decisions. The ability to make the right decisions comes from having made the wrong decisions. —HSRjr*

Do you want to earn money, or do you want to make money? To play on the words of the previous lesson, the "average thinking" person will tell you that making money and earning money are both one and the same. An "active thinker" who also has an entrepreneurial mind-set and spirit will tell you different. As an "active thinker" with an entrepreneurial mind-set and spirit, I am telling you that they are not the same. I learned the difference between the two when I read the book "Rich Dad, Poor Dad" by Robert T. Kiyosaki.

The most important lesson throughout the book was that there is a fundamental difference in thinking, understanding, and teaching between the rich, the middle class, and the poor. It is this thinking, understanding, and teaching that is passed down throughout the generations that keep the rich getting richer, the poor getting poorer, and the middle class just struggling to keep their head above water.

As I stated in a previous lesson, Mr. Kiyosaki's "rich dad," who was his best friend's father, taught him how to view wealth differently than his real father, who was his "poor dad." When he decided at a young age that he wanted to be wealthy, he began to follow the teachings of his "rich dad," while at the same time learning the value of a good education from his highly educated but "poor dad." Although his "rich dad" did not possess the level of education that his real father had, he did possess a great deal of real estate and businesses all over Hawaii.

In short, his "poor dad" banked on gaining a solid education, getting a secure job, and then hoping that upon retirement the government and the job would continue to take care of him; however, his "rich dad" believed that it was more beneficial to create and own businesses and own real estate. His "rich dad's" philosophy was to have the money from those ventures create newer ventures then be able to live off of the money made from those ventures as opposed to waiting for or expecting the government to take care of him. "Rich dad" believed in making money while "poor dad" believed that true security was to be gained by increasing one's level of education, which, in turn, would increase one's earning potential.

As I began to learn and incorporate the lessons I was learning into my life, I found myself getting very excited. I knew I wanted to ... I knew I had to do something beyond my chosen profession in order to secure wealth for myself and my family. So, I spoke with my wife, Taria. I shared with her what I was learning and even asked her if she would like to read the book when I was finished with it. However, I should have known that she would politely decline because she's more of a hands-on, arts and crafts, right-brain type.

Me, I'm more the analytical, logical, left-brain type. So, I asked myself, "How can I get her to learn what I'm learning if she won't read what I'm reading?" Then it dawned on me—I had to make what I was learning palatable for her. I had to convert what I was learning in books into something tangible that she could put her hands on. Knowing that she loved taking pictures, I asked her what was there to stop her from starting her own photography business. Then when I knew I had her attention, I dug in harder and deeper. You see, if we are dedicated to nothing else, we are dedicated to our family, and I knew that would have to be the leverage I needed to inspire her to learn what I was learning. So, I shared with her the lesson I learned about the difference between earning money and making money, and if you will indulge me, I would like to now share that lesson with you.

When we go to our jobs and punch that clock, at the end of the week, we get our paychecks. That is money earned. The problem with earned money, however, is before we get our hands on any of it the government has already gotten its cut right off the top. Now, if you can create a product or service where there was none—or improve upon something already out there—and have people find so much value in that product or service that they will pay you what you charge for it, then just as you made that product or service, you have made money! One day she accompanied her father to a wedding that he was being hired to shoot video of the event.

She went along and took pictures that would be incorporated into his video. When the couple got the pictures, they paid for from their "professional" photographer, they were less than pleased. So, they asked Taria if they could see the pictures she took. She made a brief slideshow presentation for them on her laptop, and when she gave the couple her price, they jumped on it, and when she presented them with their wedding package, they practically wanted to adopt her.

The end result: Taria realized that she just made money and it felt great! After a couple months of her doing a little bit of business research and developing her business plan, we went to our accountant and made Personal Touch Photography a real, live entity! Her goal now is to be able to leave her regular nine to five and strictly do photography within the next two to five years.

(www.TariaReed.com)
Yes … I know it's a shameless plug!

In April of 2006, some two or three months after helping Taria get her business started, I had an epiphany. I knew I wanted to create my own business, but for some reason I just could not put my finger on what it was going to be. After a period of reflection and also while continuing to read book after book after book, I realized that over the years I have always been a person who friends could call upon to get genuine and unbiased advice. I have always been the type of person who would tell a friend what they needed to hear as opposed to what they wanted to hear.

Also, I always felt the need to want to help them come up with solutions to their problems. I never professed to have all of the answers, as my life has had its fair share of setbacks and obstacles, but I always sought out solutions, and that was how I decided to become a motivator, an "investor in the human spirit!" Inspiring my wife to start her own business and actually make money at it was my first success on my journey of becoming a motivational speaker.

It not only gave her a new sense of purpose, it actually made me decide I would create my own business as a speaker. I figured if I could use what I learned to help myself and her, I could also inspire others to find the greatness that exists within themselves. My first professional speech was at the 2006 eighth grade graduation ceremony of the school I attended as a child. The principal there today is the same one I had as a student there. When I asked if I could address the students and their families at the ceremony, I specifically stated I did not want to be paid; for me it was about giving something back to the school that helped mold me by letting those children see and hear from someone who sat in the exact same classrooms they sat in.

If there was any selfish motive, at the very least it would be the experience gained by giving the speech. So, I wrote my speech, rehearsed it, and presented it to a crowd of close to two hundred people. At the end of the ceremony, the principal's secretary gave me a "thank you" card. Inside that card was $150 cash. From what I learned, I had just proven for and to myself what my wife had already proven. I spoke for twenty minutes and made $150. I felt great! I was on top of the world. I had become a legitimate professional speaker! All kinds of thoughts and images ran through my head.

The most important thing that stuck out in my mind was when I started crunching numbers. You see, I looked at it like this: if I was worth $150 for twenty minutes, then I could be worth at least $450 an hour— not bad for a novice, right? In any case, at that point, it wasn't about mapping out how much I could charge in the future, but I was reveling in my present success and the possibilities of the future. As a firm believer in karma, I believe that what you put out in the world will come back to you—and sometimes five- to tenfold.

Just so you know, when I got that unexpected $150 from my very first speaking engagement, I donated half of it to the local Toastmasters chapter that I joined. Sometimes you can give money. Sometimes all you can give is your time but give something. There are times I will just say something nice to a stranger walking down the street or standing in line at the grocery store. Remember, the universe is always watching.

When I first released the first copy of this book, I did not have the resources of a publishing house's marketing department. Almost every copy I sold was practically sold from the trunk of my car. Other sales were at speaking engagements. There were times when I left the house with just a couple of dollars in my pocket but came home with a couple hundred dollars. The fact that you even have this book in your hands proves the difference between earned money and made money.

I am still a police officer and will be—God willing—until I retire in 2025. My salary is my "earned money" for the work I put in every day. I appreciate the fact that you found enough value in it to purchase it. What can you do that you could possibly turn into a business for yourself? What can you do that you enjoy that you can also profit from? You see, experience has taught me that no matter what it is, if there is something out there to be sold, there is also someone out there willing to pay for it. For my wife, it is her skills as a photographer. For me, it's my skill as a speaker and an author.

Whenever we go to the movies, turn on our CD players or our iPods, we have hundreds of examples of people who have created something that we have found enough value in to spend our money on. However, at this point, what is even more important to me is that you commit to your personal success— right here and right now. The lessons in this book are the lessons I have learned that have gotten me where I am today, and as long as I live true and strong to those lessons, I cannot go anywhere but up. I am on my journey, and I am committed to my personal success.

You must be committed to yours. This book is my commitment to helping you along the way. With that said, this is where we shall soon begin to part ways. Keep in mind all that you've read came from someone who is just as normal and regular as you are. Then again, if you are an "active thinker" like I am—or after reading this book you become one—you will find there is absolutely nothing "normal or regular" about you.

I can assure you that if you apply yourself to yourself and never give up you will achieve your goals. If you remain true to yourself and the ones you love, you will have great relationships be they romantic or just regular bonds of friendship. Have faith in yourself. Know what you want and set your goals accordingly. Hold yourself accountable when you falter. Be the first to acknowledge your transgressions and then work to atone for them. Success in both life and love is a journey, not a destination to be reached.

### Lesson Six: Money is an Idea

### What limits does an idea have? —HSRjr

Say the word money. Say it again—money. One more time … with some feeling now—money! Now, take a look at yourself. You feel good, right? Every time you said the word money, I'll bet the majority of your thoughts and inner dialogue was positive. Maybe you thought about a fancy car or a big house. Maybe you thought about buying a nice gift for your husband or wife or everyone that you care about. No matter what it was, for you individually, the reason why you had positive thoughts about money was because of how we said the word both individually and collectively.

Had we gone about saying the word money like it was attached to a steel girder on one end and to our necks on the other end, we would all probably be sitting here thinking about how high that electric bill is going to be after we take down all those Christmas lights or the hole in your wallet after doing all that Christmas shopping … Oh my God … let's get away from that—quick … repeat after me …"money!" Take a look at a dollar bill. That dollar bill is not money. Oh no—that dollar bill is a form of currency, and there is difference between the two. You see, currency is merely the tool we use to manifest our ideas into reality. With that said, if you limit your reality to the currency in your pocket or bank account, then that will be the parameters of your reality, otherwise known as "living within your means."

However, I want you to ask yourself a question just for you to file away and pull up later on. What limits does an idea have? One day one of my coworkers saw me reading a book, and upon learning that it was written by Robert Kiyosaki and Donald Trump, he said to me, "You don't wanna be rich. Rich people have nothing but headaches." Now, even though this happens to be someone I genuinely like and respect, when he said those words to me, a funny thing happened.

I realized I was learning from two wealthy men how to go about expanding my ideas, while my coworker was encouraging me to narrow my ideas. Then I thought to myself, "Hmm ... do I want to learn from people who are where I want to be, or do I want to learn from someone who is pretty much right where I am and totally content staying there?" I'll tell you what—if rich people have nothing but headaches, they can surely afford the best aspirin on the market!

Being that this is not a book about personal finance or wealth building, this particular lesson is going to be very short. However, what I want to get across to you is that money is an idea. Its manifestation is a direct reflection of how great or small your idea of it is, as well as how hard you work (or don't work) to bring that into reality. Big ideas accompanied by big effort will produce big results.

Likewise, small ideas with little or no effort or the search for a quick buck will produce equally small results. Even with so-called "fast" or "easy money," if you have little or no appreciation for the process with which it was made, well, like the old saying goes, "A fool and his money are soon parted." For three years I told myself that I could not afford to buy a house. The truth of the matter is I probably spent half of that time falsely comforted by a self-induced, narrow-minded lie. I say this because in less than six months after changing and expanding my ideas about what I could afford, I was able to buy my home.

As I have stated before, I am no better than any of you. I am just a man voicing an idea, but just as we all had positive thoughts about money based just on how we said the word earlier, I submit to you that if you make a conscious effort to expand or demolish the limits and boundaries you have about your ideas about money, you won't have opportunity knocking at your door— you just might have opportunity knocking down your door!

*(Author's note: When this book was originally written, I believed Donald Trump to be an intelligent businessman. In 2016, that belief changed. I personally believe the man is a total fraud and disgrace to this country. With the exception of mentioning him above, all other commentary about him has been removed from this edition.)*

## Lesson Seven: Compound Reading

***The more that you read, the more things you will know. The more that you learn, the more places you'll go. —Dr. Seuss***

One of my favorite television shows is The Cosby Show. Many people criticized the show saying that it was "unrealistic" for a successful African American doctor to be married to an equally successful African American lawyer and for them to have five well-balanced children whose mistakes were typical and relative for mistakes made by kids of their ages. Bill Cosby played the "imperfect dad" rather perfectly. There were times when he was the "cool dad," and there were times when he was the "strict dad," and there were times when he was the humorously "embarrassing dad"—which is kind of like when he was trying too hard to be the "cool dad" but in doing so would just go to show just how out of touch he was with what was current.

The fact of the matter is, as much as I admired Mr. Cosby's portrayal to a rather high standard of comparison, I compared him to my dad. I remember one episode when Cosby's (T.V.) son, Theo, was describing one of his classmates. He was saying that his classmate was so deep into his schoolwork that if when studying one book the author referenced another book he would read both the original book and the book that the author referenced. Now, although Cliff Huxtable was impressed by such studiousness, I, like many of you who may have seen that episode, thought, "Who in their right mind would want to do that?"

If you never saw that episode, you've probably just asked yourself that very question now. Now fast-forward to 2006. Early in the year, I began reading Robert Kiyosaki's Rich Dad, Poor Dad. While reading that book, he referenced a book called The Richest Man in Babylon by George Classon. I thought back about that Cosby Show episode, and I wondered what would happen if I tried reading a book referenced from another book. It turned out to be one of the best decisions I ever made! It was somewhere around that time that I made a conscious decision to put my PlayStation down and start picking up books.

The next thing I knew, I was reading two books simultaneously. As a matter of fact, I read The Richest Man in Babylon from cover to cover before I finished reading Rich Dad, Poor Dad! The Richest Man in Babylon is a book that teaches about the benefits of saving your money and paying yourself first—and benefit I did. I was so moved by it that I set it up for 10 percent of my paycheck to be automatically transferred into my savings account every payday.

Several months later, I was involved in a car accident. Between my insurance deductible and car rental while my car was being repaired, I had to come out of pocket to the tune of just over $900. Guess what? All I had to do was transfer that money from my savings account back into my checking account and cut a check.

I had the money right there on hand, and it did not upset the regular flow of paying for my regular expenses. In short, I benefited from making a conscious decision to take action and implement into my everyday life that which I was learning from those books. I even created a new motto for myself: "Get your mind right/get your money right." Just reading those books and the others I read throughout the year was what got my mind right. Actively implementing what I was learning is what helped me get my money right. By the end of 2006, I read a total of thirteen books.

In 2007 I read sixteen books, and in 2008 I read fifteen books (it was a hard year). I am still reading more than one book at a time. I have to tell you I cannot think of very many better activities than reading. It saddens me to see so many people have such a lack of appreciation for reading. The only thing sadder than a child who can't read or cannot read well is the sight of an adult who cannot read, or at the very least read well. A child not encouraged to read is destined to become an educational casualty as an adult.

When my niece Bryanna comes to visit, she's required to spend at least an hour a day reading. My wife, Taria, sometimes tells me I'm too strict, but I made it a point to explain to Bryanna that I don't want for her to be in her thirties when she discovers the value of being well-read.

If at ten years old she can begin learning the value of reading and enjoy the broadening of her already blossoming young mind, when she becomes a woman, she will be that much stronger in a world that does not take it easy on the unfit and uninformed. When you eat, you are providing your body with nourishment. When you eat healthy foods, your body lasts longer and grows stronger. However, if your diet consists of junk food and an overabundance of greasy fried foods, your body will deteriorate a whole lot sooner than you would like.

Likewise, when you read healthy motivational and constructive material, your brain receives nourishment, and if you read garbage … well, the best way to describe the outcome is in old computer programming lingo: GIGO (Garbage In Garbage Out). Taria thrives on audio books. She listens to them on her way to work, while at work, on her way home from work, and while she works on her computer at home. Personally, I cannot get with audio books. I'm just an old school throwback I guess. I just have to have that book in my hands. It's like I am feeding the material to myself instead of having it fed to me. However, I do very much enjoy listening to seminars that have been recorded to cassette or CD.

Every day, thousands of people improve themselves intellectually by forgoing morning and evening drive-time radio programs and listening to different audio programs. Some people have learned to fluently speak several languages by listening to the necessary tapes or CDs. People have gone so far as to learn the skills necessary to improve and or change their careers or even start their own businesses! In fact, one of the great things about this book is that it's also available as an audio book!

The most important thing is that you feed your mind quality information and also implement what you learn into your everyday life (unless you have a thing for reading books about crime and/or the macabre). Even if the only types of books you like to read are fictional stories, you will—at the very least—improve and increase your vocabulary.

*Every man who knows how to read has it in his power to magnify himself, to multiply the ways in which he exists, to make his life full, significant and interesting. —Aldous Huxley*

Additionally, reading does not have to take up a great deal of your time. People tend to have a disdain for recreational reading because of the trauma that arises when they remember all of the reading they were forced to do while in school. When I made the decision to put my PlayStation down and start picking up books, one of the reasons why had to do a lot with the quality of how I was consuming my time. I had some games that I would actually spend two, three, up to six hours playing in one sitting.

I cannot remember when exactly, but I remember once asking myself, "What did you gain? What are you walking away with?" I even used to joke with my wife and describe my game time as "saving the world." When I told her that's what I was doing, she knew I was in front of the PlayStation! It did not matter if I was a spy on a one-man suicide mission, the leader of a Navy SEAL team in a steamy South American jungle, an ace fighter pilot destroying every enemy jet in the sky, or some martial arts warrior fighting mutant demons from another dimension—if I did not have to go to work the next day and I was up late, before going to bed, my wife would yell downstairs, "Don't stay up all night saving the world!"

Actually, I am half ashamed to admit that there were more than several "all-nighters" committed to "saving the world." This was why I began questioning the quality of my time consumption. I may have gotten an immediate thrill from playing those games—and that's just what they are designed for. However, a year and a few months later, I can honestly say that I am far better off for having committed more of my leisure time to reading than to satisfying the PlayStation, Nintendo, and X-Box gods!

*A man practices the art of adventure when he breaks the chain of routine and renews his life through reading new books, traveling to new places, making new friends, taking up new hobbies and adopting new viewpoints. —Wilfred Peterson*

Again, reading does not have to take up a lot of your time. Just like a decent exercise program, you can pack a quality mental workout in twenty minutes, and over the course of time you will have created a cumulative effect of "mental" improvement. Why did I call this lesson "Compound Reading"? Well, let's examine what happens if you set aside just twenty minutes for reading (quality constructive material):

20 minutes x 30 days = 600 minutes or 10 hours per month

10 hours x 12 months = 120 hours per year

Although I cannot recall his exact source, I do remember hearing Les Brown say that if you were to read one book per month in a given area, within five years' time you could fall somewhere in the top 5 to 10 percent of the most knowledgeable people in that area. How well could you improve your career if you were among the top 10 percent of the most knowledgeable in your field? What if you actually hate your job and want to venture into another field?

This book did start out acknowledging that we wanted to go about making changes and improving our lives, right? Hey ... if ever there were a secret to finding a way to make a way, that secret would lie in the pages of just about every piece of quality motivational reading you could get your hands on!

My wife, Taria, continues to hone her photography skills by reading (and listening) to books and even watching instructional seminars on DVD. Her top goal and priority is to generate enough photography business so that she can quit her nine to five and become her own boss. This brings me back to a point I made earlier—you have to implement what you learn into your everyday life.

***Unless and until you do something with what you have learned, you might as well not have learned it. The person who won't read is no better off than the person who can't read. —Zig Ziglar***

Overall, this book was written with two main objectives for you:

1. Discover the greatness that exists within you. (Find a way)

2. Take immediate action to manifest that greatness into reality to improve every area of your life. (Make a way)

Reading, in my humble opinion, is the best catalyst for such a transformation to take place and for these objectives to be accomplished. You see, when you read, you open your mind to new points of view. To use a cliché, you "broaden your horizons." When you have a wider and broader view, you also have more options. More options give you more avenues you can choose from to take you to the improvement and success you want for your life.

If reading one book increases your knowledge, then reading an additional two or three books that inspired or assisted in the writing of the initial book you're reading could very well increase your knowledge two- to threefold. So, this brings us full circle right back to The Cosby Show episode about young Theo Huxtable's friend. Although completely fictional, like most fiction there is some semblance of reality in it. In fact, a great deal of The Cosby Show came from Mr. Cosby's life as a husband and father. "Hanks," the maiden name of his "TV" wife, Clair, is in fact the maiden name of his true wife, Camille. As we all know, the Cosbys were also the parents of five children. So, was art imitating life?

Perhaps, and if so, it must be equally easy to believe that there are in fact parents somewhere out there in the world who are very much capable of instilling extremely good study habits in their children at home, such as those habits exhibited by Theo's classmate. I know with all that I have benefited from the art of "compound reading," I shall surely instill such a study habit in my son. As I am writing this book, I am thirty six and he is four. Imagine the head start he will have over me! I have learned a great deal from having immersed myself in reading; consequently, by actively implementing that which I have learned into my everyday life, I was able to improve not only my life but that of my wife, Taria—and my young son, A.J.

In fact, what started as a letter to my son has evolved into this book, and in writing it, it is my hope that you too can better yourself in the same way I have done so for myself.

The biggest tragedy in the world is not the great waste of natural resources, though this is tragic. The biggest tragedy is the waste of human resources. Many people die with their music still in them. Why is this so? Too often it is because they are always getting ready to live. Before they know it, time runs out. —Oliver Wendell Holmes

I have succeeded not because you bought this book but because I am sharing my experience with you, because I am sharing the sources of my motivation with you, and because you will (hopefully) take action and improve your life and the lives of those you love. I have made a conscious decision that I will not be one of the average people that Oliver Wendell Holmes has been quoted as saying goes to their grave "with their music still in them." When you pick up and read a book (or even listen to an audio book), you are feeding yourself a mental meal.

Remember, just as your body reacts in accordance with how you feed it, your mind operates in the same fashion. As a matter of fact, considering that it's the mind that controls the body, you might want to consider being twice as cautious about your mental diet as you are about your physical diet.

### *Where Do I Start?*

Guess what? You already have! That's the beauty of reading. You might not know exactly who the best sources to learn from are, but if you pick up one good book (like this one), you're going to be given a great many sources to check out. Anyone who claims to be any kind of authority in any area must validate himself or herself by citing credible sources. Either somewhere throughout the book the author will mention other books, or there may be footnotes or even a bibliography at the end of the book (all three apply with this book).

From reading the books in Kiyosaki's Rich Dad, Poor Dad series, I was motivated to read The Richest Man in Babylon by George Classon. From listening to and reading Les Brown and Anthony Robbins, I was turned on to the great Zig Ziglar, who with over thirty years' experience in the arena of motivational speaking and personal and professional improvement can be best described as the motivator's motivator!

There is no right or wrong way to expand and improve upon reading. George Lucas, the creator of the Star Wars franchise, wrote a dynamic six-part story about war and peace and good versus evil but started telling the story (on film) with episodes four, five, and six. He then filmed and told stories one, two, and three some twenty years later, and the overall story never skipped a beat. I am not suggesting that you pick up a book and start from the middle. Now, I am not saying that you should pick up a book and start reading it from the middle then back to the front (unless you have a thing for Quentin Tarantino movies).

What I am saying is that you can pick up any book anywhere, learn which other book or books inspired that first book's creation, and then read those books too! In the beginning of this book and throughout this lesson, I acknowledged some of the people I have learned from. Some of them I hope to actually meet before my life's journey comes to its end. As for those who have already gone, I shall certainly see them when we are both sitting on a cloud looking down upon you and yours. At the end of this book, I will share with you a list of books you can acquire on your own in order for you to take your life to the next level.

In closing this lesson, I want you to understand that the beautiful thing about this is that there is no time limit. There is absolutely no pressure—except that which you place upon yourself. The hardest thing to do is to take action, to take the first step, and guess what? You have already done it! If you take it upon yourself to read any of the books on my list or of a list of your choosing—and/ or then decide to read the many other works of those authors—you will be like Theo Huxtable's friend. You will be like me—you will be a compound reader!

*The only difference between where you are right now and where you'll be next year at this time, are the people you meet and the books you read.*
*—Charlie "Tremendous" Jones*

## _Epiloque: The Secrets To Success Revealed!_

By now, I am certain you have realized that there are no magic genies anywhere to be found who are just waiting to grant your every wish, but there are millions of "magic lamps" out there in the world. You can find them in your local libraries and bookstores. All of the "secrets" to success are in books, and I am humbled and honored to be able to add this book to that gathering. It is imperative you understand that whatever it is you want to achieve in life, you can.

There is no need to try to reinvent the wheel, but hey—if you believe you can—go for it! After all, there would never be Ferraris, Porches, and Lamborghinis if there was never the Model T! There are millions of coaches for you to learn from out there, both in print and in people. At this point in time, I would like to share with you the titles of my "magic lamps." They have brought me all of the success I enjoy today, and I am completely certain that if you apply yourself and totally commit to your success, you too will be able to overcome the obstacles you may have once thought would hold you back for the rest of your life.

Believe me when I tell you that if you read these books and make a conscious effort to take active steps toward improving your life by implementing the lessons to be learned, the few dollars you will have spent on these books (including this one) will prove to be the best investments you could have ever made in your life! From this point on, consider yourself promoted to the position of president, chairman, and chief executive officer of "You Incorporated." This company has the potential to go all the way to the top, provided it is managed properly. Guess whose responsibility it is? That's right—yours!

### My "Magic Lamps"

**The Courage to Live Your Dreams** by Les Brown

**It's Not Over until You Win** by Les Brown

**How to Win Friends and Influence People** by Dale Carnegie

**The Richest Man in Babylon** by George S. Classon

**Reallionaire** by Dr. Farrah Gray
(Self-made millionaire by the age of fourteen!)

**The 48 Laws of Power** by Robert Greene

**Think and Grow Rich** by Napoleon Hill

**Rich Dad, Poor Dad** (the entire series) by Robert T. Kiyosaki

**Unlimited Power** by Anthony Robbins

**Awaken the Giant Within** by Anthony Robbins

**The Art of War** by Sun Tzu

**Better Than Good** by Zig Ziglar

**See You at the Top** by Zig Ziglar

**Over the Top** by Zig Ziglar

**Jeffrey Gitomer's Little Black Book of Connections: 6.5 ASSETS for Networking Your Way to RICH Relationships** by Jeffrey Gitomer

**Create Your Own Future: How to Master the 12 Critical Factors to Unlimited Success** by Brian Tracy

**Where Have All the Leaders Gone?** by Lee Iacocca

# _Success_

_To laugh often and much; to win the respect of intelligent people and the affection of children;_

_To earn the appreciation of honest critics and endure the betrayal of false friends;_

_To appreciate beauty, to find the best in others; To leave the world a bit better, whether by a healthy child, a garden patch or a redeemed social condition;_

_To know even one life has breathed easier because you have lived._

_This is to have succeeded._

_Bessie Stanley—1905_

## Message in This Day

*What is today telling you? Instead of feeling that you must fight against the events and developments of this day, decide to carefully listen.*

*Imagine that there's a message in each circumstance that comes your way. Proceed as if you're receiving valuable information that can make a real difference in your life and in your world.*

*Instead of becoming completely consumed by what's happening, take a moment to consider why. Then go one step further and look at ways you can make use of the new knowledge that is coming your way.*

*The challenges that arrive, the joys you experience, the disappointments, the discoveries, and the seemingly random happenings all add up to something. Let go of the need to instantly jump to shallow conclusions about each little thing and seek to know the whole picture.*

*Find out for yourself what happens when you make the assumption that everything occurs for a reason, and that those reasons are good. Take a step back from what seems to be turmoil, observe with your heart, and you'll begin to see order.*

*Choose to see the message that today is bringing. And you'll find in it real treasure.*

*Ralph Marston*

## A FINAL WORD...

Please do not think I am some superstar hotshot just because I have written this book. I am simply a man who has taken stock of himself and decided that the best way I can repay my Creator and the universe for all of the blessings I have received is to share my stories and my experiences in the hopes that people like you can and will commit to your own success. I learned that if I did not commit to my success no one else would, and if I were to become a failure in life, I would have no one to blame but myself.

For me, failure is not an option. I will accept a setback, but I will not accept failure. I can overcome and recover from a setback but not a failure. Failure results from not doing what you knew you should have done but chose not to do. Again, failure is not an option. Originally, this book was supposed to be a letter to my son. It was supposed to be a letter that contained some ideas, opinions, and observations, but as I wrote, my ideas, opinions, and observations expanded and became too big for them just to be shared with him. One of the things I am most concerned about is what will be said about me after I have passed on.

What stories will people tell about me? What good did I do? I am quite aware of the "not so good" things that I've done in my life, and I'm sure when I'm facing my "final judgment," I will be reminded of them, but what I want to go to my grave knowing is that I have given something of value to the world be it an encouraging word to a friend or a word of advice to a teenager who is at a point where he or she could go right or wrong in life. I want my name and stories about me to be synonymous with words like discipline, honor, and integrity.

I believe there is greatness in everyone. I also believe that most people are too lazy to tap into that greatness, which is why there are so few people who are considered successful in relation to those who are not. Those of us, yes, you too, who are willing to draw a line in the sand and instead of daring the universe to cross it jump across it ourselves are the ones who will live life with passion and excitement! If this is the first motivational book you've read, I implore you that you not let it be your last! As I said, there are millions of magic lamps in the form of books that are out there just waiting to be rubbed. If you don't find what you're looking for in one book, look for it in another.

That's the beautiful thing about reading; even if you find you don't like what you've read, you've learned what not to look for in your future reading material and are more inspired to find something that better suits your taste. No matter what, from this day on, start realizing you are either part of the solution or part of the problem. Start taking stock of yourself. Plan your work and work your plan.

Share in your successes, learn from your setbacks, and if failure should come across your path, don't beat yourself up (or allow anyone else to)—just hold yourself accountable and fight on! Finally, after you've succeeded, be it great or small, find a way to make a way to give back. Remember, the universe is watching, and if it sees that you are squandering your success, you will find yourself by yourself asking, "What happened?" With that said, I wish you success. I wish you joy. I wish you all that you deserve out of life! God bless.

Wherever you are in your life today, it is a result of the quality of the foresight you had for yourself before today. If your foresight lacked quality—or worse, you had no foresight at all, the only thing that you will be able to clearly see is whatever exists in your hindsight.

**—H.S. Reed, Jr. Investor in the Human Spirit**

Made in the USA
Middletown, DE
14 March 2023

26666221R10126